The exploration of human Consciousness...
...is the essence of human life.

THE CONSCIOUSNESS GAME

When you read this book, it stays with you.

SHIKHAR SRIVASTAVA

Published by

Invincible Publishers

Published by
Invincible Publishers
201A, SAS Tower, Sector 38, Gurugram – 122003
Phone: +91-124-4034247, +91 9355675555
www.i-publish.in

First Published in 2020

ISBN: 978-93-89600-65-0

Disclaimer

This book is a work of fiction. All the names, characters, incidents, places and events are entirely fictional and are the product of the imagination of the author. Any resemblance to actual events or places or persons is entirely coincidental. The references in the book are used in a purely fictitious manner and are not intended to harm, disrespect, defame or derogate any person or authority.

Tribute

"Nature is God in its very real existence. It is the fulfiller of all your prayers, it is the answer to all your problems. It is the beginning of the enigma of life and it is the conclusion of every quest. Nature is the reason the cycle of birth and the law of karma exist. Nature is the reason that you want to possess and indulge, that you want to be born again or live forever. It's the keeper of the deepest secrets. It's the provider of great treasures. There is nothing more divine than what we can experience with our senses, nothing more pacifying or more mystifying than the natural surroundings. It is the protector and the punisher. It is the mother and the child."

In Memory of...

My Father,
Who lived his life inspired by a Mystical Universal Code.
The Code where faith & hope supersede planning.
The Code continues to inspire.

Dedicated to...

My Mother,
For believing in me, from the time, when I was too young to believe in myself
My Wife Shilpi,
For being my Friend, Companion, and Inspiration
My Son,
For being the miracle that you are

With blessings from...

The 'Flotilla' of amazing people who influence my life in very special ways
(Sagar, Shashank, Neha, Poorva, Minni, Misha, Sarthak, Rohan, Prakamya, Mansi, Tushar, Vishal, Gudiya Jijji, Saakshi, Sameer & Bindu)

And Special Thanks to...

Those who spent their time and courage in reading my initial drafts
(My Father -in-Law, Nambiar Sir, Santosh, Shivani, Meghna & BittooJijji)

With all Culminating to...

GOD (Finite and Infinite)
The dilemma of your creation... is the quest of my life

YOU ALL MADE IT HAPPEN!!

Content

Preface 1

Part 1 – Man (Purusha) 7

Raghu : My First Death 9

Shiv: Chakras And Nadis 14

Rohan: the Coincidences 23

Vani: The Shree - Yantra 30

The World Of Energies 40

Nature's Law Of Originality 46

The Sinister Plan 57

The Mystery Of Lord Ram's Story 62

The Third Eye Coverup 66

Ghosts Of The Past 79

Parallel Universes 82

The Life - Changing Decision 90

The Mystery Of God Pictures 100

The Consciousness Rnanubandhanan 109

Part II– Nature (Prakriti) 115

The God's Dilemma 116

The Fourteen Worlds 124

The Map Of The Universe 134

The Virtue Of Human Stupidity 146

The Fight Between Good And Evil 151

The Hidden Message 161

The Final Quest 170

The Guru's Wisdom 173
The Granthi's 180

Part III – God (Purush+Prakriti) 185

The Panch Kosha 186
The Rise Of The Asuras 196
The Power Of Sound 200
Water Has Memory 206
Heart Vs Brain 208
Ego 220
God 231
The Awakening 244
Afterwards 249
Bibliography 252

PREFACE

Who am I?

I mean, what is 'I' ? What is it inside of me that actually makes the 'I' in me?

Let's try to decipher this. Here I wish to tell the readers that I have liberally used 'I' and 'Me' as interchangeable words throughout the book.

All the religions of the world converge at two points of agreement:

- There will be 'something' left of me, the 'I', when the human body will die.
- And that 'something' will be rewarded or punished based on the actions that I perform in my human life.

To put it simply, religions dissect my physical being into Mortal and Immortal parts named Body and Soul respectively.

There is a Supreme Power called God, which will punish or reward the Immortal part of Me.

I find it ironical that the Immortal part of me works throughout its lifetime to nourish and pleasure the Mortal part of me which finally dies, and my Immortal part will be punished by God for the sins of indulgence enjoyed by the Mortal part.

Human Body is the most exquisite mystery of Nature. Millions of cells and thousands of body parts work in perfect symphony to enable us to perceive nature and interact with it and yet, Life as we know it, is administered by unknown mysterious forces unperceivable to the human body.

Thoughts, emotions, attachments, feelings, love, anger,

happiness, sadness, memories etc. are all the unseen and unknown mysterious forces which create the perceptionof life.

We can program a robot with Artificial Intelligence to perform all the actions of a human body, but it cannot be programmed to Meditate because it is hollow from inside. It is not administered by the mysterious life forces. There is nothing inside to talk to.

But 'I' can meditate. I can talk to the Immortal me inside my Mortal Human Body.

Amidst all these revelations, I was still missing a point.

A point which shocked me upon its discovery!

The point was that there was never a Mortal part of me. It was always dead. There was only one me; the real me—the Immortal me.

Who am 'I' ?

I was left wondering, is my perception of reality actually the reality? Or is it just a web of Karma; a game that is being played by a higher self around which all the life is revolving?

The mystery deepens when we understand it from the point of view of Consciousness. The inner voice which guides every life on Earth controls the game.

We all play this Game knowingly or unknowingly. Where strangers come in contact with each other in a twist of coincidences and affect each other's lives in ways unfathomable to human understanding. Where the results of our past actions affect our present and shape our future. Where we unwittingly give into the hands of fate and destiny.

UNDERSTANDING CONSCIOUSNESS

The Vedic literature conceptualizes God as an absolute, infinite, formless and timeless Sea of Consciousness called the *BRAHMAN,* also known as *PURUSH.* Let us understand Brahmanas–an infinite ocean of spirits.

Creation begins when out of this infinite ocean, a tiny droplet measure of spiritenters the Magical Box of creation called *PRAKRITI* or NATURE.

But there are certain Laws of Nature that everything entering Prakriti has to follow. The foremost condition being that to enter Prakriti one has to be Created or in other words, has to take Birth.

To take Birth, the spirit has to surround itself with a *SHARIRA* or BODY. So, Sharira becomes the Created and takes Birth.

Now, the interaction of Spirit with Prakriti happens in two stages:

- At the first stage, the Spirit interacts with the Body by means of **CONSCIOUSNESS.**
- At the second stage, the Body interacts with Prakriti by means of ten Indriyans or Dasindriyans.

BRAHMAN

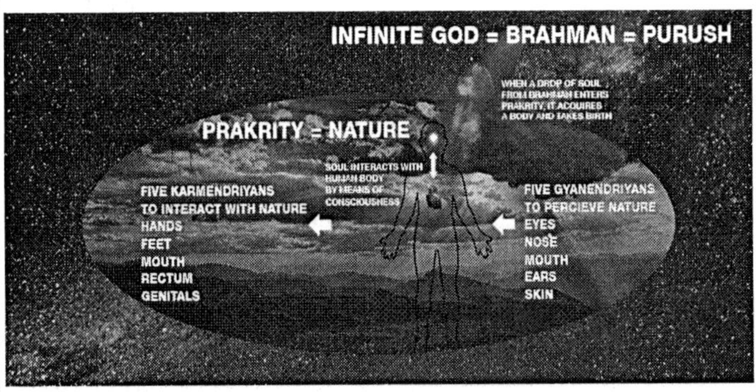

The Dasindriyans can be classified into two types:

- Five Sensory Organs (*Gyanindriyan*) which include nose (smell), eyes (see), mouth (taste), ears (hear), and skin (touch). These are sensors or five entrance doors with which all living beings perceive or collect information about Nature or Prakriti as they call it.
- Five Actuatory Organs (*Karmindriyan*) which include feet (for walking), hands (for holding), mouth (for speech), rectum (for excretion), and genitals (for reproduction).

Karmindriya means organs of action which facilitates human interaction with Prakriti or the material world by performing actions.

Whenever a human body performs any kind of action, it is said to have performed a *KARMA*.

So basically Karma is any kind of interaction that the human body has with Prakriti. Every Karma is an action and it leads to certain reaction. Simplifying it means every deed performed by a human being will lead to certain dividends. Karma says 'as you sow, so you reap,' meaning every action will bear the fruit of Karma which will be a matching outcome of the type of Karma. On the basis of these reactions, Karma can be classified into three types:

- Satvik Karma or Good deeds - Leading to positive effects.
- Tamsik Karma or Bad deeds - Leading to negative effects.
- Rajsik Karma or Neutral deeds–It has neither positive nor negative effects and is done purely to enjoy the fruits of Mother Nature.

By the end of human life, we can metaphorically say, that the statistics of Karma of life are displayed like a bar - graph with a bar each for Satvik, Tamsik, and Rajsik Karma.

If the bar for Satvik Karma is high, one will go to heaven and stay there till the meter again resets to zero. Likewise, if the bar for Tamsik Karma is high then one will go to hell for the duration till when his sins purify and the meter again resets to zero.

After that, this spirit will be born again and again in 86 lakh Yonis in one of the six life forms namely aquatic animals, plants, insects, birds, and animals before being born as a human being again.

Since only human form has been blessed with free will and choices, the principle of Karma applies only to human life. The rest of the life forms are only driven by their primal instincts and are not affected by the Laws of Karma.

This infinite cycle of births and deaths continues till a Soul decides to utilise a human life in pursuit of knowledge that can free it from this misery. Liberating oneself from the confines of this box of creation called Prakriti and again uniting with the Infinite Sea of Consciousness (Brahman) is termed as Moksha.

Consciousness is an entity that facilitates interaction between a spirit and a human body, so as to help the human body in pursuing its true purpose in Prakriti. It is widely acknowledged to be an inner voice that guides a person towards Satvik Karma.

The human history is replete with incarnations of God who took birth in flesh and blood and performed miraculous deeds. These incarnations were spirits enclosed by a body akin to any other human form and bound to abide by the Laws of Nature. The difference was that Gods were guided by Gods' Consciousness and humans by Human Consciousness. In other words, Gods had more knowledge about their true self as compared to humans; this knowledge was imparted by none other than Consciousness.

Let us unfold this mystery of Consciousness; a mystery when solved can change the very perspective of looking at our human body and our understanding of the game of destiny that governs the life of every single living being in Prakriti. Let us decipher the deepest secrets unknown to mankind despite lying in open view.

Imagine Consciousness to be a real entity; an entity that can think and guide a human being. Imagine it to be a formless bluish glow that is present inside the human brain and guides the human brain to perform Karma by means of the

Dasindriyans.

You might just rule it out as a figment of my imagination, but isn't everything in the world just a figment of human imagination? Countries don't exist in nature; they are demarcated by human imagination. The entire economic system that governs human lives is also just defined by human imagination. The law system, work culture, religions, and even God exists because humans believe in these imaginations deeply.

When you imagine something deeply, it becomes your reality.

Imagination is more powerful than the reality that we live in because our reality is just the amount of nature or Prakriti that we can perceive with the help of our five senses; whereas imagination has no such restriction. Imagination can transcend all barriers and make anything possible.

I am Consciousness, and this is the story of my transition through four human bodies and my discovery of the secrets that will turn me into a superhero and will finally lead me to uncover the greatest mystery of all—God.

PART 1 – MAN (PURUSHA)

CHAPTER 1

RAGHU : MY FIRST DEATH

I was first born as a formless bluish glow, surrounded by darkness inside a human head.

The human brain was there in front of me under a layer of reddish glow and appeared to me to be two quarter - spheres kept adjacent to each other with a network of thin veins and neurons within which numerous random electrical discharges were taking place.

Ten bluish rays were coming out of my body with five falling on the left quarter - sphere of the brain and five falling on the right quarter - sphere of the brain. I was guiding the ten Indriyans of this person with the help of these ten rays acting like my hands.

As the person (in whose body I was born) opened his eyes, the darkness inside his head disappeared with the appearance of a bright scene in front of me. For a moment I was lost at the sight of all the light and colours that appeared. Then, the colours began to merge to form shapes.

Through the eyes of my human body, for the first time I witnessed Nature. The sensation called life cannot be explained; it can only be experienced.

It was as if I had woken up from a night of eternal sleep and realized my true self. Or was it that I was awake earlier and now, I was having this beautiful dream called lifewhich appeared to be so real that it made me forget about my true self?

Whatever it was, it was mesmerising.

The colours, the fragrance, the taste, and the vibrancy around all which is defined as Nature, was so strikingly gorgeous that if this was a dream I would prefer to stay in this dream state forever; and if this was what they call life, I would want to be an Immortal and live forever.

It took me a while to realize that I had an identity separate from the human body I was residing in.

The memories stored inside the brain of this human body served as a ready guide for me to understand the identity of this human body. I was guiding the brain of a person called Raghu, who was travelling in a car along with two more friends in a city called Mumbai in India.

The scene I was witnessing through Raghu's eyes showed his two friends sitting on the front seats of a car and a long road was to be seen through the front glass of the car, at the far end of which, a girl could be seen standing at a bus stop.

'Let's do it,' the person sitting on the driver's seat spoke.

The person sitting on the co - driver's seat took out three injections filled with a yellowish liquid and distributed it amongst them.

The moment Raghu injected himself with the liquid, what happened was instantaneous and catastrophic. I felt weak as if someone was suffocating the life force out of me and my control over Raghu's Indriyans weakened.

'Ready, guys?'said the person sitting on the co - driver's seat. 'I will stop the car in front of the girl standing at the bus stop. Raghu, you pull her inside and Aftab, you inject her with the drug. Then, she is ours for the night'.

Since I am the Consciousness, people generally acknowledge my presence when, either they are passing through a personal tragedy or are about to commit a sin. I can only be heard by those who look for answers within themselves rather than those who choose to exploit nature to rid them of their miseries. I grasped that, in this case, Raghu was about to commit a heinous crime. 'What are you going to do? Rape her?' I yelled at Raghu, shuddering at the thought of the crime that was about to happen.

'There is no harm in having fun sometimes.' Raghu's thoughts echoed inside his brain as if he was speaking to me. 'I will make sure she is not left in a condition to tell anything to anyone afterwards.'

'Raghu,that is not what human life is meant for,' I said, shuddering at Raghu's animalistic arrogance. 'With human life, you can experience love. You can bring a smile on a girl's face, win her affection, and you can experience life in a way that cannot be experienced even by angles. Why do you want to destroy your and someone else's life? You have got a chance to live the most beautiful creation of supreme almighty, don't ruin it.' My voice was breaking down as the effect of the intoxicant was increasing.

Just when I thought I could convince Raghu to withdraw from the felony, something dramatic happened inside his head. The mild reddish glow over Raghu's brain turned redder and took the form of a horrific, small reddish figure.

It was identical to me and hadtwo hands just like I did, made up of reddish rays with five fingers in each hand, which joined the brains exactly where my fingers were touching the brain. With each passing second, I was getting weaker and this figure kept on getting stronger and stronger. Soon, it was strong enough to overpower me.

'Who are you and why are you doing this?' I asked the reddish figure.

'I am Raghu,' the reddish figure said in an authoritative voice.

'But so far, I thought I was Raghu and I was guiding his actions,' I said.

The reddish figure didn't pay any attention to my words. It kept growing in size and kept on strengthening its hold over Raghu's brain.

The woman standing at the bus stop was a tall and beautiful girl in her middle age. She had a height of about 5' 9 and was wearing a salwar suit which had specks on it. Her hair were tied in a ponytail and she was carrying a lab coat which was hanging from her arm. Her attire conveyed that she had just returned from her workplace and was oblivious to the intentions of these miscreants ogling at her.

In my last desperate attempt to prevent the mishap from happening, I cried to the reddish figure,' Look you can save this. You don't need to do this. After all, like me, you also must be a creation of God.'

The reddish figure grew larger in size, turned back, and in a devilish tone said,' I have not been created by God; I am a product of the human brain. I am Ego.'

The car was hardly 15 meters away from the unsuspecting woman when suddenly there was a loud horn. A speeding truck screeched as it braked and impacted the car with such ferocity, that it sent the car flying up in the air. The car landed upside - down on the road.

The woman standing by the side of the bus stand was the first to arrive on the scene of the accident. She was a nurse in a nearby hospital. She immediately called for an ambulance.

Of the three people sitting inside the car, the two sitting in the front were fatal casualties. Raghu, sitting in the rear, was still breathing when the nurse pulled him out of the car, loaded him into the ambulance, and attended to his wounds on his journey to the hospital.

I saw glimpses of her angelic face in the traffic lights during the road journey. I saw the reddish figure disappear in obscurity without any trace whatsoever as she bandaged his wounds to control the bleeding and implored Raghu to hold on with his life for only a while more.

I saw tears rolling down Raghu's eyes as she placed her hand on Raghu's forehead. He had been driven by an animalistic desire to ruin the life of this divine woman who was now nursing his wounds to protect his life.

A moment had changed everything.

She will have to attend to Raghu tonight. She might get late at work and be compelled to travel alone tonight. She might again have to face the eyes of such predators that lurch with the desire to take advantage of the darkness around them to conceal their misadventures.

Raghu–the Body, Raghu–the Ego, and Raghu–the Me, died a little while later.

My first realisation of the Miracle of Nature had ended due to the desire of a mortal body to wilfully ignore me in pursuit of a misdirected and destructive aim.

But, what I had failed to comprehend until now was that this event had put in motion a complete cycle of Karma that will unfold in times to come and will reveal many secrets which will enable me to discover a new reality about myself and God.

Raghu died but I was still alive.

I was the Immortal part inside Raghu.

The CONSCIOUSNESS GAME had begun.

CHAPTER 2

SHIV: CHAKRAS AND NADIS

I woke up again in a completely new body.

Strangely, in this new body, I felt the presence of a mysterious energy all around me. I felt more powerful.

'Hello there, I have been waiting to talk to you.' The surroundings echoed with the voice. It was as if this voice just knew that I had arrived.

'How are you aware of my presence inside you?' I asked.

'Well, the only thing that I am aware of is whatever goes on inside my head. Of course, I know you. You are my creation– my inner voice,' the man said.

His answer perplexed me for a while. He was right. From his point of view, I was his creation as he was not aware that I already had an existence independent of this body. From his point of view, I was just a voice inside his head, an integrated accessory that comes along with the human body at the time of birth.

'Well, you are right in a way. So firstly, let me compliment you; you have a very open mind,' I said, to keep the communication going.

'Haha! I don't know about that, but maybe that's why people call me crazy,' He said.

'Crazy? But why? So far you seem to be normal to me,' I said.

'That's what the society calls people who are born autistic, 'He said.

'Autistic?' For as long as I could remember, it was the first time I had encountered this term.

'Yup, do not sound confused. I can't exactly tell you what the society means by it, but maybe I can express myself and I don't seem to deal with society the way normal people do,' He said.

For a moment, I was muddled. What did he mean?

I quickly reached for his brain and placed my 10 fingers to gain control of his senses. His 5 sensory organs or Gyanindriyans seemed to be working fine. His 5 actuator organs or the Karmindriyans also seemed to be working fine. There was no visible symptom that I could find which could differentiate him from any other mind that I had encountered.

However, there was a catch and it struck me.

There was a huge variation in what is termed to be 'normal'. He had an abnormality with regards to the energy flow in his body.

Contrary to human belief about the functioning of the human body, I learnt that the human body, just like a machine; has its own system of energy generation and distribution.

Like how plants can directly harness solar energy for their survival, human beings too have been blessed with several such energy engines by which they can receive energy directly from nature and process it for use by the human body. These energy engines are called Chakras.

Although texts differ with respect to the number of chakras in the human body, a common understanding evolved in the present era enlists seven main chakras located along the spinal cord in the human body as the most important ones. The seven chakras are as below: -

- Muladhar Chakra or Root Chakra
- Swadhishthan Chakra or Sacral Chakra
- Manipura Chakra or Solar Plexus
- Anahat Chakra or Heart Chakra
- Vishuddhi Chakra or Throat Chakra

- Ajna Chakra or the Third eye Chakra
- Sahasrara or Crown Chakra

Each chakra is associated with a peculiar colour, sound, and shape. When a person meditates, a dormant energy called Kundalini Shakti rises up like a serpent from the Muladhar Chakra and opens up the channel of energy flow as it passes through each chakra.

Once the energy has been supplied through the chakras, it is circulated throughout the body with the help of 72,000 nadis out of which the three most important ones are:

- **Ida Nadi** - Ida Nadi is the lunar or feminine Nadi and corresponds to the left side of the body and the right side of the brain. It controls all mental processes. Maybe that's why when I touched the right lobe of the brain, I gained access to their Gyanindriyans.
- **Pingala Nadi** - Pingala Nadi is the solar or masculine Nadi and corresponds to the right side of the body and the left side of the brain. It controls all vital physical processes. Maybe that's why when I touched the left lobe of the brain, I gained access to their Karmindriyans.
- **Sushumna Nadi** - Sushumna Nadi runs between both the above Nadis along the vertebra. It is essentially a vacant space. But when Kundlini Shakti rises through it, it opens up all the chakras one by one, leading to the attainment of Siddhi of Supernatural Powers.

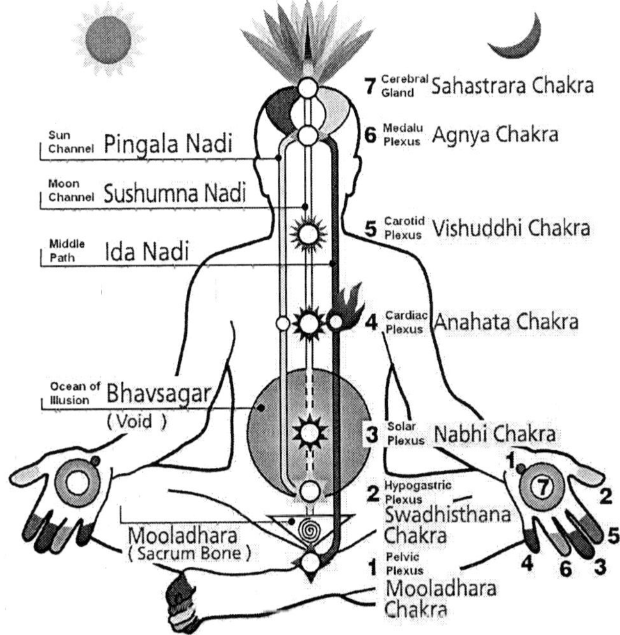

Energy Centres & The Subtle System

There is also an auxiliary source of energy. It combines the entire digestion process which has been designed to harness energy from nature by first consuming natural things and then treating them with various chemicals inside the stomach to finally harness usable energy from it. In the process, a lot of waste is produced. This process is responsible for ageing and diseases in the human body. It is ironical that human beings work throughout their life on a process of survival which will finally age and kill them.

But I soon discovered that the reason for this outrageous human stupidity is simply that a majority of humans are incapable of using these chakras as the primary source of energy.

This is because at the primary level, the human body is not ready to handle the huge influx of energy that each chakra can bring.

Every chakra is associated with a special kind of energy that is provided to the human body to achieve a special Siddhi. If the human body is ready and the person has learnt to use any one of the chakras, then he can attain siddhi to perform deeds which may be considered miraculous by the human world, as it will defy the physical rules known to them in the four - dimensional world.

The human body is made up of incredible wonders. It is the most amazing creation of God, but every human has not been blessed with the wisdom to extract the full potential or even experience that infinite vastness enclosed within the confines of a human body. One can say there is a kind of safety mechanism incorporated in the human brain which limits their ability to deny the unworthy access to this out of the world wisdom.

A person's capability is only narrowly defined by his physical structure. Human capability is actually all about his ability to channelize his energy in the correct direction.

This new body I had acquired differed from others in a very special way. This person's Ajna Chakra, also called the Third Eye, was partially active and generated three times more energy than any other normal person. As a result, his mind was functioning faster than his body. It could have been manifested as a supernatural gift but his body was not ready to handle the unknown frequencies of this extra energy.

The distribution was also a problem. Ida Nadi was carrying more energy generated from Ajna Chakra as compared to the Pingla Nadi. This had created a dissymmetry of energy balance in the body.

As a result, the person had difficulty in coordinating his normal vital physical functions which were controlled by Pingla Nadi. The coordination between the brain and the body was disrupted and thus, the person had inadequate control over his five Karmindriyans.

He was mostly confined to an electric wheelchair and could painstakingly use his hands for bare minimum activities like eating, wiping etc. He was able to see and sense but could hardly communicate in a language comprehensible to the world.

On the other hand, the extra dose of energy provided to the Ida Nadi had provided him with supernatural mental capabilities. But without the capability to decipher or express what he was experiencing inside his head, his power was nothing but an abnormality.

His physical disabilities had made him a perceived liability and led to his boycott on the social front. Maybe that was the reason that led to him being abandoned even by his parents when he was just one year old.

His past life was a secret. He had been told that he was raised in an orphanage in Mumbai till an NGO adopted him and under the pretext of nurturing specially - abled people like him, the NGO secretly sold him to a pharmaceutical company based in Mumbai.

Under the cover - up name of a pharmaceutical company, this company used to manufacture narcotics and drugs and needed a human body to test their products. My new human body perfectly suited their requirements.

His body responded to the effects of these drugs and he neither asked for compensation nor was there any chance of him leaking the information about the injustice done to him. For the last twenty years, the pharmaceutical company was keeping him captive at a forlorn location near Shimla and used him as a subject for testing their drugs.

'What's your name?' I asked.

'I am Shiv,' He said.

Whenever Shiv spoke to me, for any third observer looking at him from outside, he must have seemed to be in a state of deep meditation or mumbling something.

'You might be cursing yourself for being trapped in my body. I can't move a limb.' Shiv said with a sarcastic smile.

'Look Shiv, I see a lot of potential in you, but you need to help me to understand you 'What? Why? Why suddenly? What's there in Shimla? you completely because your body is very different from others. First, tell me how you learnt of my presence in your body?' I felt a deep connection with Shiv.

'It's the drugs—that pink serum that they had injected me with,' Shiv said. At first, I was shocked to hear that, but slowly I figured out.

The human brain is like an antenna that operates in different bandwidths of frequencies. There is a human bandwidth which includes all the visual and audio frequencies within the spectrum of bandwidths required to operate bodily functions like smell, touch, dreams, energy flow, etc.

As there is a spectrum of human bandwidth reserved for humans, similarly, there are bandwidths reserved for the animal world, spirit worldand the world beyond. Human beings can slowly train their mind to operate in the bandwidth beyond the human spectrum by means of meditation. An alternative way of making a brain lose control over the frequency spectrum of the human body is by injecting it with chemicals called drugs.

Under normal conditions, the human brain can catch only those frequencies usable by the human body. But whenever the brain is under the influence of drugs, it loses its control over the confines of its operation. Its thinking can transcend into unknown realms and dimensions. A typical drug - addict describes visualising light, colours, and several out - of - the - world phenomena; these are nothing but the extra frequencies his brain is catching under the influence of drugs which are beyond the human spectrum of frequencies.

Only through proper meditation, a person can fathom what exactly he is looking for in the infinite scope of the human mind.

However, with Shiv it was different. His brain could function on unfathomable frequencies.

Initially, whenever Shiv was injected with drugs, he could neither control nor understand what was happening inside his brain. Slowly, after repeated undertakings, he began to understand the familiar spaces and developed an understanding of this supernatural territory.

This misadventure, with the normal functioning of his brain, had done severe damage to his health. His bones and muscles had weakened and his vision had blurred slightly. While he was only 22 years of age, he looked much older.

'You have come late. I am a prisoner here; just a subject of experiments. My destiny is to die in this chamber,' Shiv said.

'Our destinies our connected,' I told Shiv, there is no me without you and there is no you without me. You are my identity today Shiv and I assure you, I will find a meaning to your life. This cannot be the end. Whoever God is, he has written every single life as a beautiful story and I will not let your life end as a tragedy.'

'Tomorrow they are coming to inject me with some new, experimental drug that has been perceived to be dangerous. I don't know if I will survive that.' Shiv startled me.

'Then we have very less time,' I said. 'First, I will have to get you out of here. We need to get outside help,' I started planning.

'Do you mean you want to contact other bodies you are connected with?' Shiv asked.

'What other bodies?' I asked, 'Am I not your Consciousness and limited to your body?'

'You are my Consciousness, not some part of my body that you will be confined to the physical boundaries of my body,' Shiv said.

The idea of looking beyond this human body had never occurred to me. I had a feeling that my pairing with Shiv would be interesting.

'How can you be so sure that I am connected to other human bodies?' I asked.

'I am not sure, but I feel so because I can connect with other human minds. I think you are that connection,' Shiv said.

'You can connect with other human minds!' I asked in bewilderment, 'How is that possible?'

'There is a science called Telepathy by which a person can

communicate with another person who is sitting in some other part of the world by using only mind waves. The human mind operates like the internet. Every mind is connected to all other minds like the computer nodes of the internet. If one can connect to the correct router, he can reach the other minds connected to the web. I have myself traversed through many brains when I'm in my deep meditative state. I can teleport you into someone else's mind, but what you do after that is up to you,' Shiv said.

'I understand it now; you have a partially active Ajna Chakra or the Third Eye that has the power of telepathy. Maybe, unknowingly you have activated that power. So, hurry up! Telepathy me!' I commanded with excitement.

'You mean, teleport you? You want to leave me and go?' Shiv asked.

'No Shiv, you have no idea about what we are going to achieve. I can be back to your mind any time you need, but with your help, I can go to any mind that I desire. You mentioned something about the internet web. Well, every web needs a server or a master computer. You are that server to all the minds connected with me,' I said.

'But what will all this lead to? What will happen by your going to other minds?' Shiv asked.

'Coincidences will happen,' I said.

CHAPTER 3

ROHAN : THE COINCIDENCES

Coincidence is a grossly misunderstood situation. People have a perception that coincidences are incidents that just occur by chance; hardly do they know about the huge number of divine forces and the precise calculations that are involved in making coincidences occur.

Coincidences are those junctions where life paths of different people intersect for a bigger purpose. They are a part of a grand plan played in perfect symphony to achieve a larger than life objective. They are turning paths in the lives of people that can catapult them into unchartered territories and completely transform their lives.

The discovery of telepathic powers by Shiv in itself was an accident that was sure to trigger off a series of coincidences.

When the eyes opened, I saw a rickety shed with a variety of broken vehicles all around. Everywhere that I could see, it was just machines and their parts. Shiv had teleported me into a person named Rohan who was fixing a truck when I spoke to him.

Rohan belonged to Goa. To pursue his passion about cars, he had moved to Vaishali in Ghaziabad (which is located near the border of Uttar Pradesh and Delhi) where his friend, Santy, owned an old, motor garage which was destined to be the temporary research facility for these newbies.

They had bought the chassis of a vintage Chevrolet truck and refurbished it with a Toyota 4. 7L V8 tundra turbo diesel engine and large - sized Goodyear tyres which had wide dimensions of 66 inches by 43 inches. The result was a gigantic, red - green monster chassis with six rooftop spotlights, and seemed to be hung on the four, strong, shock absorbers over the tractor - sized tyres.

'We need to go to Shimla…a friend needs us,' I whispered inside Rohan's head. The best part about being Me is that I can just start a conversation without the customary mandating of the initial introduction. Somehow, everyone knows me when I awakens inside them.

'Santy, I feel that I need to go to Shimla,' Rohan said to another boy working next to him under the mounted truck.

'What? Why? Why suddenly? What's there in Shimla?' Santy asked.

'I don't know, I just feel something…maybe it's just a glitch but I feel I need to do it,' Rohan said with an unresolved tone.

'Then, let's do it, brother. There's still six months to the Tokyo motor show, I think I should take a two - day vacation,' Santy said with a smile on his face.

'I have a plan. Let's drive down to Shimla, our monster truck is also ready, and it can be a trial run. It's just a 9 hrs drive from Delhi, it should be good,' Rohan said.

For the last one year, Rohan and his partner, Santosh aka Santy, had been working on an all - terrain vehicle that could participate in the prestigious Tokyo motor show held once in every two years in Tokyo.

Rohan and Santy reached the outskirts of Shimla at around 7:00 am the next morning, where they took a break for having breakfast at a small, road - side restaurant.

'Are you still connected to me, Shiv?' I asked in wilderness and was delighted to get a reply.' *How can I leave you?'*

'Tell me what all can you see outside the window,' I asked.

'It's just pine trees all around and a broken signboard showing the way to L&T holiday home,' Shiv replied.

'Santy, I think we should go to L&T holiday home which has pine trees around it,' Rohan said.

'What?' Santy asked, with a half - chewed *aloo parantha* in his mouth.' Why? I have had only one *tandoori parantha*, I need at least four. I have been driving all night, and why L&T all of a sudden? Are you hiding something from me?' Santy asked in a suspicious tone, with a raised eyebrow.

'I don't know. I am just following my instincts, maybe we will have fun there,' Rohan said.

'But I am having fun here also, *tandoori parantha* with white butter is the epitome of fun for me. Besides, knowing how you are, I am terrified of your eagerness; it can land us in thick shit like many a times before...' Before Santy could complete his sentence, Rohan had already begun to lurk around.

Rohan asked the people around but no one seemed to be aware of any L&T Holiday home. Then, he searched for it on Google maps and was able to locate one, but it was not in Shimla. It was near a place called Kufri which was located at a one - hour distance from Shimla.

The drive to Kufri was a little bumpy, but once they were clear of traffic, the huge wheelbase worked phenomenally on those broken, mountainous roads. Rohan took a detour from the main road near Mashobra, to drive on a broken, single - lane road covered with forest all around.

'Bhak...Bhalu...Bhal - ku...It's Bhalku Road. So, now we are truly off - roading. It is good that I packed a few tandoori *paranthas* for the route,' Santy said and took out a rolled newspaper packed with *paranthas* from his pocket.

Suddenly, Rohan hit the brakes and the truck screeched to a halt at a completely desolated spot in the middle of the forest.

'It is strange,' Rohan said.' Although it is the first time I have come to these hills, I feel as if I have seen this place. '*The place had the same trees that Shiv had watched from the window.*'

'Now you are scaring me, buddy. I have the right to be pre - informed if I am being led into a ghost - hunt. I know the law, it is a human right to be informed about one's death due to stupidity,' Santy said with a smug, keeping the *paranthas* back in his pocket.

'Let's go up that hill, we might get a better panoramic view from there,' Rohan said, without paying any heed to Santy's concerns.

I could sense that Shiv was close - by, but I didn't know which direction to take to reach him; when, in between the hills, I saw a lonely, rickety hut with pine trees all around it.

'I think we should check out that hut,' Rohan said.

'It sure looks like a haunted house; who are you hoping to find there? Everyone in your family is alive; it can only be related to your last birth. Bro! I don't want to die a virgin,' Santy said.

'Relax, we are just having fun,' Rohan said,' but I will get the lug wrench from the truck, just in case.'

'I am not going inside; in fact, I will sit on the roof of the hut. God knows what is going to come out of it,' Santy said while trying to climb on top of the roof of the hut.

'Wait... wait, let me help you,' Rohan said and began to support Santy on his shoulders.

At 97 kgs, Santy resembled a genetic - cross between Santa Clause and Humpty - Dumpty, and his innocent smile on his chubby face perfected the look. It took almost superhuman strength in Rohan to lift Santy's gigantic bums over his shoulders and push the centre of his gravity over the slanted roof of the hut.

Once relieved, Rohan moved towards the door of the hut with the iron wrench in his hand. The hut was made up of temporary wooden planks and was not as small as it looked from far. In fact, it looked as if it had more than one room.

The door was latched from inside. Rohan slowly moved around the hut to find a window which was partially open.

'This is it, I have found the place. Shiv just hold on for a few more

minutes,' I thought.

'I need to go inside,' Rohan thought and peeped inside the window to find a pale figure lying on the bed and two tall figures standing next to him.

One was a thin guy with a wheatish complexion. He was wearing a colourful shirt, with the top two buttons of his shirt open and his chest hair jutting out. He had a dreadful and expressionless face, with a scar stretching from the top portion of his nose till under his left eye. The white powdered residue under his nose signalled frequent snorting of cocaine. My interaction with Raghu had taught me a few things about these substances called drugs.

'Monty…get hold of the fuckin retard,' the thin guy commanded the other tall, muscular guy who had tattoos all over his hands and neck while signalling towards Shiv. 'This time the stuff is strong; boss told to check if a little extra dose can be fatal. There were complaints of a few people dying. Let's see if this bastard can take it.'

'Bhatta! I will be more than happy if he dies; it will at least save our effort of repeatedly coming here,' Monty said while lifting Shiv and placing him on the bed.

Then, he attached an ECG machine and a pulse meter to Shiv and took hold of an injection with a pink serum inside.

Just as he was about to inject the drug into Shiv, there was a loud cracking sound.

'What is that?' Bhatta yelled.

At the same moment, Santy came crushing down from the rickety roof and landed right on top of Monty, squashing him under his weight toppling the bed on which Shiv was lying. Monty fell unconscious due to the impact.

Bhatta was aghast for a moment but quickly recovered to pull out a .45 Colt pistol from the holster tied to his waist.

He was Shivering with anger when he pointed the gun at Santy and shouted, 'Who the fuck are you?'

'Tourist!' Santy replied in a pleading voice while raising both his hands.

'You bastard, how did you reach here? Before I kill you, tell me who has sent you? And what is that packet you are carrying?' Bhatta said, pointing to the roll of newspapers that had fallen out from Santy's pocket.

'It's... it's nothing. It contains *tandoori paranthas* that I got packed,' Santy replied and tried to reach out for the roll of newspapers.

'Stand still you rascal, you think I am a fool,' Bhatta yelled, and get away from there. 'I don't want the bullet to pierce through you and kill that retard or Monty; step to your right.'

Santy slowly got up and moved to his right. 'Please don't kill me, I mean no harm,' Santy said.

'Too late for that, you don't know with whom have you taken *panga*,' Bhatta said, moving the Colt to point at Santy.

Suddenly, the conversation was interrupted by a loud roar of diesel engines, a monster truck bulldozed the sidewall of the hut and smashed Bhatta into the opposite wall.

'Just in time,' Rohan said, 'get in quickly. We need to get out of here.'

'Good Lord, I don't believe I am alive. Let's go,' Santy said while getting inside the truck.

'Wait, we should carry that pale looking fellow also, I think he is alive,' Rohan said. In that moment, Santy just followed whatever Rohan was saying, there was no time to argue.

Rohan was reversing the truck when a loud bang from a pistol muffled the engine noise momentarily and a bullet broke the right rearview mirror of the truck.

Rohan pressed the acceleration and sped down the hillside, gaining speed, with the truck tyres crushing the bushes. Rohan could just get a glance of the blood - covered face of Bhatta before he got out of sight. The truck didn't stop until they reached Chandigarh.

'He is alive and very angry, they can trace us if he would have seen our number plate. We may have to get out of Delhi for some time,' Rohan said.

'What do we do with him?' Santy asked, pointing at Shiv.

'Can't leave him, he has all the answers; he will have to go with us. There is only one safe place that I know of,' Rohan said.

'But where can we go apart from Delhi?' Santy asked while unwrapping the *tandoori paranthas*.

Rohan kept on driving without replying. Santy knew the answer. The monster truck headed to Goa.

CHAPTER 4

VANI: THE SHREE - YANTRA

The coastline of Bandra in Mumbai, is known as the 'Queen of Suburbs' for a reason. It houses the residential and business complexes of some of the biggest business tycoons of India.

At the early hours of dusk, in one of the tallest buildings on Bandra skyline, a tall, muscular figure stood on the top floor looking out of awall - sized window at the sunset.

He was bald and had a grim, expressionless face. He was dressed in a formal black suit and shiny black shoes that exuded richness from every quarter.

With the knock at the door, a formally dressed man hurriedly entered his office. 'We have found the location, Boss. Somewhere near Cavelossim beach in south Goa,' the man said.

The bald man turned back and with the same expressionless face and a deep voice said, 'Activate our Goa cell, I want my 'lab - rat' back; and whoever was responsible for stealing him.'

In two days, Rohan had hit the outskirts of Goa. He loved the sea breeze, the coconut trees, and the calmness in the air.

Somehow, Goa had remained untouched by the greedy obliteration of human ambitions. Somehow, here people valued their non - hassled living attire more than the city quackery.

Rohan felt an immediate de - slackening on reaching Goa. Everything was exactly the same as it was before he left the city about two years ago. Rohan's family owned a shack on Cavelossiam beach and ran a water - adventure business, which was solely being overlooked by Rohan's mother ever since his father died.

Rohan was able to convince his mother with a made - up story about Shiv's illness and the doctor's advice to keep him at a peaceful natural location for some time. But Rohan's mother had a strange feeling about Shiv. Despite an emaciated frame and a pale look, there was a certain innocence and honesty in his eyes that had drawn her attention.

The next morning, Rohan's mother called the boys to attend the morning prayer.

'This boy needs help,' Rohan's mother said. Santosh, help him to the puja room to attend the morning aarti, may God bless him. And you, at least brush your teeth before eating something.'

'Yes aunty,' Santy said, stuffing the half - eaten biscuit into his mouth.

'What's a puja room?' Shiv asked Santy. In the last three days, Santy had begun to understand the words Shiv mumbled.

'You don't know what a puja room is?' Santy asked, in a surprised tone. 'It is a room where they offer prayers to God. The idols of God are kept there.'

The word God struck a chord with me. It was the first time that I was going to 'see God'.

The puja room was a small room with lots of colourful pictures all around. These Gods were nothing like what I had imagined. Firstly, there were too many of them; secondly, the pictures were strangely unlike the world that I had witnessed so far. There was one God with the head of an elephant, one picture had a man with a blue body, and another picture had a scary, blue, muscular man, with long hair wearing onlya tiger skin and a serpent around his neck,with a beautiful Goddess standing next to him.

Finally,.the puja began. The ritual involved reciting few mantras and singing a few songs to please the Gods. But the Gods were just stone idols, how can a stone idol bless its devotees?

It was all difficult for me to comprehend at first until I learnt that the secret lay deep within these pictures, the secret that would make me a Superhero.

Shiv was sitting inside the puja room when there was a strange sensation inside his brain. I felt a white glow inside as if a new kind of energy was filling his mind. At a closer look, the white light seemed like a bundle of many different kinds of waves but some what different from the waves that comprise the white light of a visible spectrum.

'What is that?' Shiv asked.

I looked through his eyes to see a strange combination of squares, circles, and triangles drawn on what looked like a small sheet of metal. This combination of strange geometrical figures was kept just below the idols of the Gods in the puja room.

As Shiv was concentrating on the drawings, his mind was getting livid. His nervous system radiated tiny sparks of electricity and their vibrancy was increasing. To me, it felt as if a complete electrical powerhouse had just been short - circuited. The effect of just a sight of these random geometric figures on Shiv's mind was stronger than any narcotic he had ever been injected with.

Shiv was taking deep breaths; deeper than he had ever taken. His body started to tremble, slowly first and then, the vigour increased to a level that made him fall off the wheelchair onto the ground.

The house members were alarmed at the sound of Shiv hitting the ground and then helped him to a bed. Shiv went unconscious, but inside his head, there was a bustle of strange activity going on which was hitherto unfamiliar to me.

To understand the outlandish turn of events, I manipulated Rohan to probe the matter.

'What is that, mom?' Rohan asked his mom, pointing towards the geographical figures, knowing that she must be the best person to answer this question.

'What?' Rohan's mother asked.

'That geographical figure on a small metal sheet kept there,' Rohan said.

'Oh! That is Shree' - Yantra, it is a sacred yantra used to attract positive energies. It is very pious and this one is very old. It was given to me by my naani (grandmother). But why are you suddenly asking about that? You never noticed it all these years,' Rohan's mom said.

'No...no, just like that,' Rohan said.

'My naani used to say that Shree - Shree - Yantrahas the most perfect geometry in the world. It attracts positive vibrations. If you keep this yantra at a place, it will fill that place with positive energy,' Rohan's mother said.

Shree - Yantra was indeed strange. In fact, it looked more like some random trigonometric drawing rather than ayantra (machine). It had an outer square with a protrusion on each side of the square. Inside the square, it had three concentric circles with reducing diameters along with two layers of inner concentric circles between which petal shapes were designed that numbered 16 and 8 petals each. Inside the third and innermost circle, there were nine intermeshing triangles with five pointing downwards and four pointing upwards. At the centre of this geometry was a dot.

Sometime later that day, Rohan and Santy were contemplating the events that had taken place with Rohan holding the Shree - Yantra in his hand.

'I somehow feel that Shiv's unconsciousness has got something to do with this Shree - Yantra. I don't know what is it, but I feel there is some connection,' Rohan told Santy.

'I think he is evil,' Santy said, that's why, on entering the puja room, he felt uneasy. Evil spirits cannot enter God's residence. I don't know why we are keeping this trouble in our home.'

'I am not able to understand,' Rohan said, deeply engrossed in his thoughts. 'Can it be that a set of geometrical drawings affect the mental state of a person?'

'It is possible!'

Both Rohan and Santy were taken aback by the sound of a female voice in their reclusive chamber.

'I am sorry to enter unannounced,' Vani said while entering the room with Rohan's mother beside her. 'Aunty told me about your arrival and everything that happened here today morning and I believe, I can be of some use here.'

Vani was Rohan's childhood friend, adulthood crush, and his lifetime fantasy besides being his neighbour.

As children, they were partners of sea adventure activities and would together jump the waves on a surfer, glide motorboats on water, and sail deep into the ocean, but their favourite activity was scuba diving. Together, they had discovered the infinite wonders that the sea offered in the form of exquisite marine life, the mesmerising corals, and the thousands of species–all living in perfect harmony with nature. It was after a long time that Rohan had smelt her fragrance in his room.

'Santy, this is Vani; she is my friend and he is Santosh, my best friend. Vani has been studying the science behind sacred religious symbols for some time now. She is a professor in religious symbology.' Rohan began the initial introduction.

'I will get tea for all of you,' Rohan's mother said and left.

Vani took the Shree - Yantra from Rohan and placed it exactly on the centre of Shiv's forehead.

'It is possible for visual figures to make an impression on the mind. There is a science called Cymatics that studies the translation of sound vibrations into visible patterns. It is usually done by vibrating a fine powder or a liquid on a plate connected to a speaker. The images formed due to the alignment of grain particles with the vibrations of different frequencies passed through the plate are beautiful and astounding. Every unique sound wave produces a typical and unique image depending on its frequency. Astonishingly, most of the patterns produced on passing sound waves through the plate are perfect geometrical patterns rather than random figures.

At the basis of every yantra operation is something called 'shape energy' or 'form energy'. The idea is that every shape emits a peculiar frequency and energy pattern which is specific to that shape. Hence, a wave when passed through fine powder will align the particles of the powder into a specific shape,' Vani said.

She continued, 'The opposite is also true; when that specific shape is seen by a person, his mind will register the frequencies which are same as the sound frequencies used to create that shape. Every geometric pattern emits a specific wavelength. When this wavelength enters your eyes, its impact on your brain is similar to the one you will have on hearing the sound typical to that geometrical pattern. Have you seen a rangoli that is made outside Indian homes and temples since ancient times? It is nothing but a geometrical pattern that will instil positive vibrations in a person before entering a house or a temple. That is the basic theory on which yantra's work.'

'Apart from yantra's, there are other examples also that certify the belief of ancient civilisations in 'shape energy' - mandalas of Buddhist philosophy, the Star of David in Christian philosophy, the five - pointed star (pentagon), the Christian Cross, the pyramids and so on. Certain powers are ascribed to various shapes. Some have evil or negative energies and some have good or positive energy, but through the yantras known to us, only beneficial and harmonious energies can be drawn. Basically, yantra's are secret keys for establishing resonance with the beneficial energies of the universe.

'The Shree - Yantra is a 12,000 - year - old symbol and is considered to be the 'mother of all yantras'. In olden times, such symbols were used to balance the left and right aspects of the brain or to focus our minds on spiritual concepts to obtain spiritual benefits. It is rumoured that the great scientist, Nikola Tesla while concentrating on his experiments would see the Shree - Yantra in blinding flashes!' Vani said.

'You mean to say, that just this piece of geometry can channelize energy in a manner that can harmonise the brain, and that maybe the cause of this guy fainting after concentrating over it fora prolonged duration? Then why doesn't it happen to me?' Rohan said.

'Because every brain is different; maybe the frequency of his brain synchronised better with the frequencies emitted by the Shree - Yantra,' Vani explained.

'But even if this yantra emits some vibrations, how can vibrations affect the brain? After all,the brain is a solid matter,' Santy, who was so far quietly listening to the conversation, spoke up.

'Well, scientists today believe that matter does not exist,' Vani said.

'What do you mean? I exist or not?' Santy asked with awe.

'Once modern scientists had reached down to the subatomic stage, they were surprised to find that 99. 99% of an atom is vacant. So, how can you create a solid out of something which is 99. 99% of vacant space? To quote an example, "the total matter in the massive Empire State Building is equal to a just a grain of rice, the balance is just vacant space." What is even more surprising is that how just a rearrangement of these atoms provide completely new properties to a substance; for example, graphite and diamond are just rearrangements of carbon atoms.

If we further break down an atom, we realise that at the subatomic scale, everything is just waves. This is the basis of 'String theory' taken as the basis of modern quantum physics.

String theory proposed by scientists suggests that everything in this world including forces of nature, matter, and energies are all made up of very tiny waves resembling small strings and they all differ in their properties based on only the vibration pattern of these tiny strings.

So, if you think about it, all matter is composed of atoms and all atoms are nothing but empty spaces with a revolving electron, and these electrons are nothing but just a cluster of waves. So, in effect, matter is nothing but a wave–a concentrated bunch of frequencies.

Matter is an illusion. Just like bubbles form on the surface of water, similarly, we exist for a temporary period in this ocean of energies. Every bubble may think it is different but in fact, it is just a part of the water and connected with all other bubbles. We are nothing but a cluster of energies in this ocean of energies called the universe. We exist just like a bubble exists on the surface of an ocean - temporarily and for a limited period of time.' Vani's eloquence was mesmerising.

'Rohan! Rohan! Someone is here to see you.' The frantic call by Rohan's mother interrupted the conversation.

Rohan entered the living hall to find six tall and muscular men, including two policemen, standing in a semicircle. In the centre were the familiar figures of Bhatta and Monty. They looked at Rohan with suspicion.

'You must be Rohan Bhatnagar. Does that broken truck outside belong to you?' the policeman asked, with Bhatta and Monty watching him.

'Ah…yes…yes, that truck is mine,' Rohan said.

'We have a complaint that you have kidnapped an employee of Mr. Bhatta,' the policeman said.

'I have not kidnapped anyone,' Rohan said, 'I have just rescued a person who was being forcibly injected with some intoxicant drug.'

'Let's cut out the bullshit and get straight to the point, Where is that retarded kid?' Bhatta said, pulling out the colt. 45 pistol from his holster. The policemen just looked on.

'What is going on? Why the gun?' Rohan's mom saw the gun and cried out.

Vani and Santy also came out to the living room on hearing the commotion.

'Ok... So that fatso 'tourist' is also here,' Bhatta said, looking at Santy.

'Listen, all of you…your boy has made this issue kind of complicated. I want thatretard and I want these two to come along with me. In turn, I will do no harm to your happy family,' Bhatta said, pointing towards Rohan and Santy.

'Inspector Sahab, you don't know what these people have done to that guy. I have seen injection marks all over his arm,' Santy said.

'Inspector Sahab won't mind that,' Bhatta said, 'Maybe, you guys have not understood the gravity of the situation.' Bhatta turned towards Rohan's mother and pointed the pistol at her.

'Don't waste my time, I attach no value to any human life. Let me start by giving you an example, in any case, we will have to clean up all the witnesses of this case sooner or later,' Bhatta said.

Without any other warning, Bhatta fired a shot towards Rohan's mother's head. The bullet pierced the sound barrier to accelerate towards the target and then, suddenly, as if from mid

- air, the bullet disappeared without a trace or any scratch on Rohan's mother.

'You wanted me, you have got me! But are you sure you can handle me?' Everyone in the room turned towards the direction from where the sound was heard to witness the new entrant in the room.

CHAPTER 5

THE WORLD OF ENERGIES

Shiv was standing dressed in a white kurta - pyjama with a headband using which he had tied the Shree - Yantra on his forehead. He appeared tall for the first time, standing fully erect in his 6ft 6inch frame and his face was beaming with perfect composure of calmness and serenity. All signs of weakness in his body were gone. Shiv looked nothing short of a God sent angel at that time. He gently held Rohan's mother's shoulders and made her sit on a sofa.

Bhatta was bemused at the sight of Shiv. He had always seen him helplessly Shivering and trembling on the bed. He regained his composure and shouted at the top of his voice, 'Everyone fire! Kill all these bastards!' All six men took out the pistols hidden under their attire.

Shiv stood tall in the centre with his eyes closed. He couldn't see any person or any matter; what he could clearly visualise was the flow of energies all around him.

In the world of energies,all matter exists as a waveform and all waves travel at the speed of light. The speed of the fastest matter is negligible as compared to the speed of light and hence,time becomes relative.

In the world of energies, a fired bullet will appear as a bundle of energy moving gently in time and space; but at any particular instant of time, it will appear static.

Here, inside Shiv's head, I comprehended an entirely new perspective of creation.

The complete story of God and Creation has been converted by mankind in terms of symbols and stories, and it is within these stories that all the secrets to supernatural powers and superhuman abilities lay out there in theopen. Anyone with an open mind and a desire to learn can understand this secret wisdom to infinite power.

For example, the Trinity of Gods–this comprises of Brahma (The Creator), Vishnu (The Preserver), and Shiva (The Destroyer).

Let us try to understand this Trinity in the form of energies.

First, imagine the depiction of Brahma (The Creator). Imagine an old guy sitting on a lotus, with four heads looking in all four directions and holding the four Vedas (books of wisdom).

Maybe, they wanted to depict a set of very mild and tender form of energies that come together to form everything that we say is a part of creation. All humans, animals, plants, and non - living entities existing around us are just different ways in which these set of mild waves superimpose with each other.

Vedas are symbolic for wisdom or all the knowledge required, so that the correct set of waves are superimposed to give birth to only the desired entities.

The four heads looking in the four directions depict that creation is four - dimensional. Everything in nature is three - dimensional, comprising length, breadth, and height as the first three dimensions which together form Space, and it is further defined by the fourth dimension of Time making every entity in nature a four - dimensional being limited by Space and Time.

Maybe, that's why, despite being a part of the highest trinity of Gods, Brahma 'The Creator' is least worshipped amongst the three; because he is the Creator of an illusion of nature called Maya. He has made a cluster of energies seem like matterwhich is akin to making water statues inside an ocean. One may feel it is a statue but in fact, it is just water. Matter is an illusion.

Secondly, imagine the depiction of God Vishnu (The Preserver). The most revered of the trinity, he exists in multifarious forms. He takes incarnations to set things in a 'Natural Order' or as per Dharma on Earth. He is infinite.

Here, they may be talking about the infinite set of energies prevalent in the universe or even outside the universe that govern the laws of nature. The energy flow is not random, it takes place with detailed precision. All life forms follow certain natural rules for their life process. There is a geometric pattern that shapes all living and non - living things. Whichever Force enforces these laws can be termed as Vishnu.

His various forms are a depiction ofdifferent kinds of Forces present in nature, be it gravitation, fire, wind, water etc. But most importantly, he depicts an energy that is present in all individuals. He depicts Superconsciousness or the Soul of the universe. His blue colour depicts a kind of universality. I wondered if his blue colour had something to do with my blue colour.

Thirdly, to understand God Shiva (The Destroyer), take the complete set of energies, which are equal to Brahma energy and Vishnu energy, and reverse them in direction (in other words, put them 180 degrees out of phase). This set of energy theoretically is everything that is there in this world and yet, it is different from Brahma and Vishnu.

Imagine God Shiva: A muscular man with long flowing hair, wearing tiger skin with a snake draped around his neck, and holding a trident in his hand. Maybe, they wanted to depict a very fearsome form of energy. The snake being a symbol of Time depicts that this energy is timeless.

The fact that God Shiva sits on top of Mount Kailash may suggest that God Shiva is the powerhouse of Potential Energy with his consort, Parvati, being a sum of all kinds of Kinetic Energy. All forms of energies can be divided into kinetic or potential energies.

When this energy is let loose, it will release waves that will meet the natural frequencies of everything in nature in an opposite phase and everything will resonate to destruction. This is known as Tandav–the dance of God Shiva in which he dances to release an energy frequency that will destroy everything that exists, so that a new universe can be created.

The six men, including those in police uniforms, indiscriminately shot bullets towards Rohan's family. Shiv stood silently in the centre with his eyes closed. It appeared as if the bullets had hit some kind of an invisible energy wall and disappeared into it. Bhatta and his men were aghast at first but then they fired another round of bullets which producedthe same results. The family members were untouched by the destructive momentum stored in the speeding bullets.

The newly gained abilities by Shiv had increased my understanding of the human body. Inside Shiv's head, I knew exactly what was happening.

At a quantum scale, all Matter is composed of waves or energies only. But in the world all around us, we can touch, see, and feel matter. How is this possible?

The answer is that it has been made possible by the limitations of human senses. Humans can understand the world only through their senses,and this is possible only because human senses have limitations.

Human eyes can see only a very tiny fraction of even the known wave spectrum and humans call it the Visible Spectrum. Similarly, their ears can hear only a very minuscule range of frequencies which they call the Audio Spectrum.

Just imagine if human eyes could see or their ears could hear a wider range of the spectrum. Would their complete perception of the world remain the same then? Would your face look the same if I can see frequencies beyond the visible spectrum?

There are some animals whose audio and visual spectrum range is different from humans. That's why one can hear a dog barking or crying when humans cannot see anything, because that dog can see and hear things that humans cannot. That's how animals predict danger before time and smell their enemy much farther than any human.

Normal humans cannot see the world of energies because their brain is limiting their capacity to see beyond a very narrow spectrum of frequencies. Unlike Shiv, whose variation from a normal brain had given him abilities considered extraordinary by the human world.

To counter the hail of bullets directed towards them, Shiv simply focussed on his Ajna Chakra or the third eye to release pulses of energies which were equal to the energy carried by the bullet and opposite in phase to it. Bullets encountering these waves in mid - air resonated to evaporation, in other words, disappeared from mid - air.

Next, Shiv raised both his hands upwards as if summoning the ceiling fan and then, brought down his hands towards his chest as if holding a globe and with one rapid motion, threw the imaginary globe towards Bhatta.

All six intruders were thrown back as if hit by a speeding truck. Blood started spurting out from Monty's mouth. Almost the next instant, Shiv released a set of waves which caused unbearable headache to the six intruders.

The pain was so immense that water started flowing out of the closed eyes of Bhatta and the policemen. Shiv released his hold for a brief moment to allow the six men to escape.

There was pin - drop silence in the room at the turn of events that they had just witnessed.

'I told you he is a monster.' Santy was the first to speak.

Shiv moved to touch the feet of Rohan's mother and said, 'I am aware of what difficulties each one of you have gone through because of me. Your kindness has given back my life. I assure you that till the time I am alive, I will remain indebted to each one of you.'

'But who are you?' Santy again took the lead.

'I am Shiv, I am an orphan and so I don't know what my

beginnings were. I have no friends or family, I will narrate you my life story; whatever I know of, and also how this Shree - Yantra not only balanced the flow of energy in my body but also helped me realise the powers that lay dormant within me.'

'You are not an orphan anymore, this is your family,' Rohan's mother said.

A teary - eyed Shiv sat down to tell his life story to his new family.

CHAPTER 6

NATURE's LAW OF ORIGINALITY

At the top floor office of a Bandra skyscraper, Bhatta stood in front of a 7 feet tall, bald and muscular frame inside a luxurious floor - wide office. The bald man in rich tuxedo suit moved closer to Bhatta and asked in a calm, deep, and husky voice, 'What kind of pain did you say you felt in your head which made you run away from there?'

Bhatta was almost trembling when he uttered, 'Sir, it felt like a hundred needles had penetrated my head and my head was about to explode.'

The bald guy towered over Bhatta and held his head between his huge palms, looked into Bhatta's eyes, and said, 'A man's life is made by his decisions: had you waited and allowed your head to explode, I would have got a better idea about the powers of this new creature; you made the wrong decision.'

With that, the bald guy smashed Bhatta's head on the corner of the woodentable placed nearby. A stream of blood erupted from the corner of Bhatta's right eye. The bald guy smashed his head again and again till it was reduced to a pulp with brain splattered all over and then let the lifeless body drop on the floor.

'Call Aghora, and shoot the rest of these cowards,' the bald guy said as he moved out of the office leaving behind a blood - drenched carpet and a headless, dead body.

There had been a prevailing uneasiness between Vani and Rohan ever since they met again. Glimpses of her days spent with Rohan brought forth the fondest memories of her childhood in her mind. A lot had changed since then but despite the uneasiness, Vani still felt a kind of intimacy in the presence of Rohan.

It is a strange connection when you meet someone from your happy past. The glimpses of those happy times linger on, adding tanginess to your sober present.

The surge of emotions and uplifted mood is not only guided by a release of sexual energies as considered obvious by many who only have limited awareness about the flow of natural energies; there is but a bigger game at play on the Consciousness level.

In fact, every single person one meets in his lifetime has some kind of connection with either his past life or the future. This connection is called Rnanubandhan. It can be understood as a Karmic debt (Rnan) from the previous birth that leads to attachment (Bandhan) in this birth. Two people can be mutually attracted to one another only if there was some relationship between them in some previous life. The stage for such meetings is a junction - point where interwoven destinies meet. It is a coincidence designed as part of a universal conspiracy to add a twist to several life stories for the achievement of a larger cause.

I am what re - links these connections of the previous birth with those of the present birth as per their Rnanubandhan. Let me just keep my ways mysterious as of now. You will soon discover them.

'I waited for you...for a long time...but I heard you got married...it is good to see you now happily settled in life,' Rohan told Vani in a teasing tone while she was standing on the terrace of Rohan's house.

Vani turned as she heard Rohan's voice from behind and said, 'Sometimes destiny shapeour decisions in life and we can do very little to change them. We have outgrown the time and age of giving explanations Rohan, but I am really happy to see you after such a long time. All my best memories of childhood have 'you' in the centre stage,' Vani said, with a smile on her face.

'I think the director of this stage - play swapped my role from the hero to a side actor, now I will have to be content with watching the hero romance with the heroine from a distance,' Rohan said, continuing the flirtatious tone.

The expression on Vani's face changed. She stared at Rohan and spoke in a commanding voice, 'Bend down on one knee.'

'What? Here? On the floor...why?' asked Rohan, aghast at the sudden change in Vani's tone.

'Just do as I say. Bend down,' Vani said again.

Rohan bent down on one knee in front of Vani, with a surprised look on his face.

Vani lifted her right foot and rested the heel of her red stiletto on Rohan's thigh; then she lifted Rohan's face by his chin and bent down slightly forward to look deep into his eyes, and said 'One thing I must confirm to you; this stage - play is not a romance, it's a tragedy.' With that, she gently lifted the skirt over her right foot to expose her ankle. Just above her ankle, there was a tattoo with **Rohan's** name engraved.

'Guys, we need to move. Shiv said that those people will come back, we need to move fast and go to a safe location.' the warm conversation between the two of them had been disturbed by Santy, who was panting from running around to convey the news and had just missed a phenomenal 'gossip - sight' by just a whisker.

'But where are we planning to go?' asked Vani, lifting her feet from Rohan's thigh.

'No idea as of now,' Santy replied, staring at Rohan sitting on his knee, 'but we just need to leave this place quickly.'

'I know a place which may keep us hidden for some time,' Vani told Shiv once they reached downstairs.

'Where is that?' asked Shiv.

'I will guide you,' Vani said.

All the family members boarded the monster truck to move to an undisclosed location. Santy took the driver's seat and headed towards the Pune highway.

Rohan was sitting on the rear seat and pondering over his life.

Rohan's father owned a small water adventure club on the coast of a South Goa beach. As a child, sea adventure was in Rohan's blood but what he sought most were machines. He had developed a fascination for all things with mechanical and electrical connections in them.

Rohan was not particularly a meritorious student; in fact, he was more notorious for scoring low in most subjects than famous for scoring well in thefew subjects of his liking. But he excelled in physics. He had decided early in his life that he would choose subjects which get him closer to machines. But that was not to happen. In the 10th board examination, Rohan failed in history.

The repercussions of this failure were severe on Rohan. Apart from the humiliation, he would now not be able to get the subjects of his choice. That meant that despite being brilliant with machines, he would not pursue his dream of undertaking further studies in science because he could not cope up with history. He would now be one year junior to all his friends. More importantly, he would have to part with the most important relationship he had developed in his life until then– Vani. That entire day, Rohan hid behind a fisherman's boat kept on the beach and cried.

A student's life in India is not designed to discover talent. It has been architectured to mutilate original thinking into common beliefs because original thinking acts as an aberration to the human principle of homogeneity. A person with original thinking will stand out rather than fit in; he is more likely to question rather than obey,change things rather than follow them, so the governments devised an education system to brainwash every individual into forgetting their originality and compete with other individuals in spheres which suit their commonality.

'I am doomed. I was the biggest idiot ever; I have wasted my entire life,' thought Rohan.

'Why do you think so?' I asked the brooding Rohan.

'Because I have been a failure in my life. I was a loser in school and failed in my boards,' Rohan said.

'If it were your school grades that decided your future in this world then there was never a need for God to have written your destiny,' I said.

'Then where is God? Why doesn't he show up at such times when we need him most,' said Rohan.

'Well, believe me, I am more desperately searching for God than you are. But the fact that he exists can be seen all around you in nature itself; he always helps when you are at your weakest point in life,' I said.

'I don't know; throughout my life, I worked very hard to make my life and today, I stand with every dream shattered around me.' the man broke down and tears rolled down his cheeks.

'You see, throughout your entire life you have struggled with fear, all your decisions were guided with safety as the primary consideration. You chose a safe job, safe behaviour and tried to remain in the good books of your seniors for this reason alone; you were afraid.' this time I was confident of what I was speaking.

'That's the only way to survive. If my present and my future are not secured than how can I live?' Rohan said.

'If by survival you mean nourishing your body for 80 odd years, then maybe you are right. But do you think that is the only reason for your creation?' I asked.

'That's what everyone does. What else do we do?' Rohan was losing his control. I decided to assuage his mental upheaval.

'See, my friend, I can read your life and I must tell you that when you were born, you followed a schedule designed by your parents to inculcate good social norms. Then you followed your school's time table and then you followed the office routine. You followed the procedures, the formats, the social customs. You also followed the work and leisure setup established by countries to include holidays and festivals. All your life you have been so engrossed in following that you have, in fact, forgotten to lead,' I said.

I continued:

'God created everyone with a Unique Identification Code(UIC).

Just imagine, in tens of thousands of years of human existence, not a single leaf has ever been duplicated. In the millions of species present, not one has ever been repeated. If two water drops of the same size fall at the same place in the sand, they would still make different imprints. A person who is born today will never take birth again...ever. Even two twins will never exact.

It is the law of nature. It creates only originals. The law applies to each and every single thing, living or non - living that is a part of nature.

For humans, it means that today, on this Earth, there are more than 7 billion unique individuals. But at the same time, on this very Earth, we have only a few thousand different types of activities or jobs to be done.

It is, thus, obvious that only a few thousand can undertake the unique activity or job for which they were uniquely designed. Rest will have to forget their unique identity and follow these thousands. Now this situation gives rise to a problem of non - utilisation of their unique minds.

Suppose, in a school, in a particular class say 11th, there are 8 subjects. Now as per this law, out of 100 students, there will be only 8 students who are actually born to study those subjects; the rest 92 are born to study the subjects which have not been created by any other individual before them. So either these 92 students develop the art of suppressing their true nature and compete the former 8 students in the subjects which were designed for those 8 or accept the fact that they just can't focus their energies on that subject and be ready to be labelled as an idiot. These are the only choices available if you plan to survive in the world you have been given to live in.

So to deal with this, mankind has designed a measure of success. A person who can best suppress his true nature to fit in the norms laid down by the society is considered well - civilized and successful. Aberrations are considered unsuccessful.

Moreover, human beings have a fascination with finding commons. Their subconscious mind tries to find these commons to associate ourselves with groups. Like countries, communities, religions, groups etc.

But nature designed you to be different; every one of you. It designed you to chart an independent course. Make your own rules. Show the world the talent which only you have been blessed with.

Nature designed you to be a creator; the creator of your own world. You can believe and achieve the things you want, befriend the kind of people you want, love and marry in your original style.

The problem with following people or set actions is that though it may seem to be safe, secure, and a risk - free way of life, it is the root cause of all the boredom, frustration, isolation, and loneliness that we face in life.

Because when we follow, our mind just doesn't work. If you are following a format in your office paperwork, you will feel bored as you are just not utilizing your brain the way nature designed it to be used. You are just trying to fit in someone else's creation.

Let me put it across simply: -

- Boredom/ Frustration = Not using your mind
- Adventure/Happiness = Using your mind
- Satisfaction/Accomplishment = Successfully using your mind.

Mankind is the most beautiful and the most innovative creation of nature. They were designed to be creators and leaders, but they chose to follow.

While most of mankind spend their lives pondering over the reason for their existence, you can justify yours simply by being the creator of the nature around you.

Understand your Unique Identification Code (UIC). Be Original. Do Original. Period, I said what I had understood about mankind till then.

Rohan went deep in thought at that time. I could see the increase in his brain activity. All those arbitrary sparks were flashing randomly. I noticed a slight reduction in the mild red layer of ego over his brain. That meant that now I could more successfully guide his actions.

'But if these are the ways of nature, where does God fit in in all of this?' Rohan asked.

'I don't know. I told you, even I am trying to find God. But today, I don't have an answer.' I accepted the reality of my knowledge.

After Rohan slept, I was still toying with the idea of God when I heard another voice in Rohan's head.

'*You shall find what you seek*,' said the voice.

I looked around into the darkness inside Shiv's head and noticed another bluish glow radiating at a distance. He looked similar to me, only more vibrant.

'Who are you? And what are you doing in Rohan's head?' I asked.

'*I am what you are, I am also Consciousness but I am at a higher realm and not inside Rohan's head. I am also known as Chaitanya or Chetna, but if you want to call me by my nickname, then simply call me "Chit"*', it said.

His answer mesmerised me for a moment.

'Is it a real thing this Consciousness or just a part of the human mind?' I asked.

'*Well, what do you think? In fact, it is the only real thing. The difficult part is to understand the reality of things; that it the Consciousness that is real and permanent and not the human body,'* it said.

'I know I am real. I don't sleep and I don't die; maybe that means I am permanent but then, what is my importance to the human body?' I asked.

The gaseous figure seemed to grow slightly larger in size.' *so that means you have yet not discovered your true nature. You have the same importance that electricity has in running a fan, heat has in running a gas turbine and gravity has in the design of the solar system.*

"You don't just guide human beings to the correct path, once you know your true nature, you can invest human beings with divine powers called Siddhis that can free them from the laws of this physical world and enable them to perform miraculous feats. You can make superheroes out of human beings,' Chit said.

I was speechless at the knowledge of powers that lay within me. 'But how do I do that? How do I discover my true self and get Siddhis?' I asked.

'*You discover your true self by going beyond the unknown, by discovering God,'* He said.

Now this entire conversation was going beyond my understanding. But what this figure was saying was nothing less than a revelation for me. So I asked,' And how do I discover God?'

'*You discover God by knowing yourself. Self - realisation is the shortest path to God,'* Chit said.

'So you mean to say that God is not out in the universe; it is inside me?' I asked.

'*I mean to say that the Universe is the same, inside or outside,'* Chit said.' *Once you will understand the Map of the Universe, you will find God'.*

'WHAT? Is there something called the 'Map of the Universe' ? Whoah, this sounds incredible. You want to tell me that God has made a Map of the Universe so that people can find him.

That's unbelievable. Why would God make it so easy?' I was astounded.

'*God has always kept it easy; it is mankind that makes it difficult. Aren't there scriptures available that can assist people to understand God! Aren't there stories of incarnations that can tell people what exactly God is like! Aren't there angels that come down from time to time carrying God's messages, and aren't there human beings whose lives have been personally touched by God! A seeker shall always find God or God will find him*,' Chit said. '*You are special; what I can understand is that you have a gift*,' Chit said.

'A gift! What kind of gift?' I asked.

'*Ah, well, the fact that you were able to see me is nothing short of a miracle for your kind. This means you have already got a Siddhi. Generally,Consciousness is trapped within the dimensions of the body that he is born in.*

'*Ok, tell me how did you manage this? How did you manage to break out of the mould of the body and see me?*'the figure asked.

'I don't really know; in my previous body of Raghu, maybe I was trapped in that mould but in Shiv's body, I just felt freer to move around. Even Rohan's mind is adaptive and listens to me, thus, giving me the liberty to explore,' I said.

The figure suddenly started shaking as if all the molecules of the gaseous figure had started vibrating with a renewed energy. I think I saw a change of colour in its body.' *You remember your last body*!' The figure moved closer to me as if trying to touch me.

'*It's amazing! You are indeed special. I can read you now. You can switch bodies! That's...that's incredible. My friend, you are destined to perform incredible deeds. There must be a very special purpose for which God has made you. You have a special power through which you can switch different bodies and perfectly remember the karmas of the last body. It's a power only a few very special Consciousnesses possess. God works in mysterious ways and you are a perfect example of that. I am so happy to have met you*,' Chit said.

'So what does all this mean? I mean the question still remains. Who am I and what is my purpose? And how will these so - called gifts help me?' I asked.

'*Find your destiny,*' the figure said.

'And where do I find it?' I was still confused.

'*Ha ha...you are quite naïve, my friend. Destiny is the path God has already laid out for you. If he has given you powers, he must have decided a purpose for you. He will guide you all your life; just make sure you see his signs,*' the figure said, with an assurance that made perfect sense only to him.

'But how can I be sure that I am on the correct path towards my destiny?' I asked.

'*By making the bodies you command reach the path to their destinies,*' the figure said.

'And what will I gain by doing all this - by guiding various bodies to their so - called destinies?' I asked.

'*You will find God,*' the figure said and disappeared.

CHAPTER 7

THE SINISTER PLAN

The first sight of Aghora was a frightening one. He had long hair, braided into multiple locks, and was dressed in an all - black, flowing dhoti - kurta. He had multiple tattoos all over his body covering his entire face and was wearing a long black Tilak on his forehead. He was sitting cross - legged in front of the havan fire. The tall bald man was sitting right opposite to Aghora, on the other side of the fire.

'Marich, what you are telling me is indeed interesting,' Aghora told the bald man, addressing him by his name.' the psychic powers you have described seem amateurish, but the fact that a cripple suddenly defeated your six men without touching them piques my interest. It will be better that we go fully prepared. You just need to get your powers back, my child,' Aghora told the bald man. 'In any case, the time has come to unleash our full plans.'

'How much time until we start the ritual?' Marich asked.

'Next month's full moon will be an appropriate date. The constellations are all in place. I will prepare the sacrifice. When we unleash the spectacle, the world will get dazzled,' Aghora said.' Any news about Shiv?'

'They are on a move but we will soon have their location. Bhatta had fixed a tracking device on that truck before moving out of their residence,' Marich said.

'We will have to finish him first,' Aghora replied, 'If he realizes his secret, he can spoil things for us.'

Just then, there was a knock at the door and a suited man entered. 'sir, the subjects are ready for the final test,' the man said.

Marich and Aghora proceeded to go to an underground control room within that building. The room had a wall - sized display board that played an image of a marriage procession. Hundreds of people could be seen mingling around with each other, with ladies dressed in traditional costumes and children playing around. There was music, dance, sweets, and flowers everywhere.

'Release the sample,' Marich said in a cold calm voice.

Unnoticed by others, two masked men entered the marriage scene with a container on their back and a connected nozzle pump in their hands, disguised as an anti - mosquito spray team. The crowd chirruped in their friendly chatter, oblivious to the movement of these mischievous figures.

The two men went around spraying the substance they were carrying on their backs everywhere and then quietly moved out of the scene. The crowd continued with their normal rant.

'Get me the controller,' Marich said and an iPad encased in a hardened camouflaged cover was presented to him. The digital screen presented a user - friendly software that depicted many digital knobs with primary emotions like anger, hunger, jealousy, fear, etc. mentioned under each knob. Marich turned his finger clockwise over the touchscreen of the iPad where aknob was simmering. The digital knob captioned anger turned along with the motion of the finger to its 30% capacity. Marich then pressed a red button on the touch screen of the controller.

At the marriage procession, there was a sudden silence as if people had been stunned by some mysterious force. There was a change in the facial expression of the people. They grew angry. A child walking by a table dropped a glass. Someone yelled at the child and a group of people started hurling abuses at one other. Soon, a mob gathered and started hurling abuses at each other.

Marich increased the intensity of the knob to 50% this time.

The marriage procession turned into a fighting arena. Abuses turned into physical brawls. People grew angrier. Everyone was fighting as if they had all been possessed by demons. Men were punching women and women were beating children.

Marich increased the intensity to 75% now. Blood splattered all over the marriage procession. People killed each other like blood thirsty zombies. Everything around was being used as a weapon. Pure madness engulfed human nature as they chopped each other like maniacs. Eyes were gouged out of their sockets and ear lobes were bitten out of skulls. There were severed body limbs splattered all over the place.

Marich now increased the intensity of the knob captioned hunger and again pressed a red button.

The moment Marich pressed the button, the leftover people in the marriage procession dropped on the ground as they slipped on the splattered guts and the blood of the dead bodies scattered across the marriage ground. They then started to cannibalize on the dead lying all around.

They ate whatever they could pick up and until they vomited everything out, and then they ate more.

Marich then pressed the terminate button. The people at the marriage procession suddenly dropped on the ground as if they had been released from a spell and passed out, owing to the fatigue that their bodies were subjected to.

When they regained senses, they witnessed the goriest and most inhuman scene around them. In the last hour, they had killed and eaten their own relatives.

The evening news that day reported that out of the total of 367 guests who attended the marriage procession, 213 were dead, 93 had their limbs missing, and the balance had turned mentally unstable on witnessing the catastrophe.

'Increase the range of the antennas to 150 miles,' Marich commanded a scientist standing next to him. 'In a few days, we will enslave Mumbai, and if everything goes as per plan, then I will raze the name of God from the memory of every person on this planet.'

The monster truck halted outside an ancient temple near a small town called Gadhinglaj, located on an offshoot from the main highway from Goa to Pune.

'What is this place?' Shiv asked.

Vani stepped out of the truck and moved inside the temple without saying a word. She returned back with a man sporting a long beard and a broad smile, who appeared to be in his mid - thirties.

'Everyone meet Sarvan - my husband,' Vani said to everyone's shock.

The web of life has been woven with the thread of uncertainties. But human's discomfort, coupled with unpredictability, makes them feel scared to try anything new whose outcome they cannot predict. This makes humans live their entire lives in an eggshell of fear which they call routine.

Routine is a set of activities which give the same result each and every time they are performed. It makes outcomes predictable and removes the element of uncertainty.

This is the reason most human beings aim to establish a routine in their life as early as possible. So they go to school/college and get a job. They believe that after this, they can follow a routine their entire life. Every day they take a predictable road to office, meet predictable people, do a routine job, and come back to a predictable home life. The inability of human beings to overcome their fear and break the routine makes their life so mundane that it stops being life altogether.

The worst part about a routine is when people include other people also as a part of their routine. They want these people to act in exactly the same predictable manner to predictable circumstances, all the time.

One such routine is the institution of marriage. Instead of seeking the togetherness to explore new horizons, marriage has been reduced to a routine, formed in an eggshell of fear, wherein each partner expects the other partner to do exactly the same things every day and give the same reaction to predictable situations of everyday life. In turn, neither partner lives their life on their own terms.

Human effort to overcomethe variety and uncertainty of nature by giving a sense of familiarity and predictability to everything has taken them away from life itself. Life was meant to be unpredictable; that was the entire thrill of living.

Sarvan and Vani had undergone something like this in their married life. They were just following a routine by living together. They were neither compatible nor unpredictable. It was about three months after their marriage when Sarvan discovered that he was impotent. He could never actually fathom it during his entire childhood.

Since then it was difficult for him to have a normal married life; he found solace from his personal tragedy in his profession. The shame that he felt deep inside himself transformed into arrogance in front of his wife. They continued to fall apart emotionally. After around two years of their marriage, social considerations prevented their divorce but personal differences forced them to live separately.

'I have a reality beyond the reality in which I live today,' Sarvan had told Vani on the day of their separation. 'I need to discover my reality. What is the point of living a fake life? Let us free ourselves because only then we will be able to discover our true selves.'

CHAPTER 8

THE MYSTERY OF LORD RAM's STORY

'Would you buy a Golak Chart from me? It is for only a 100 Rupees.' Sarvan was lying under a banyan tree outside the temple when his thoughts were disturbed by the sudden interruption. A short and frail - looking hermit was standing in front of him, who had been observing Sarvan from a distance for some time without letting him noticing it.

'No baba, please move ahead.' Sarvan was appalled by the filthy looking hermit.

'If you take it from me, I will also tell you a story of Lord Ram,' the hermit insisted.

'Why? I don't want to hear any story. Please leave me alone.' Sarvan tried to shrug him aside.

'It is Lord Ram's story; every story of Lord Ram is incredible,' the hermit persisted.

Sarvan had turned into an atheist for some time now, but he was moved by the insistence of the poor hermit.' All right, baba. Here, take this money and go,' Rohan said while giving him a 100 Rupee note.

The hermit took the money carefully, studied the note, and after he was fully satisfied, took out a folded paper from his pocket and gave it to Sarvan. The paper had few pictures of Lord Vishnu and Lord Krishna and some Shlokas written on the left and right margins.

After a careless look at the paper, Sarvan asked, 'Where did you find this paper, baba?'

'That thela wala gave me *chana chat* in this for 10 Rupees,' the Hermit said.

'Wow, you ate 10 Rupee *chanas* in this and sold the paper to me for 100 Rupees. You are one hell of a businessman, baba,' Sarvan said cynically and threw the crumpled paper to a side.

The hermit quietly picked up the paper again and came near Sarvan. Despite Sarvan looking uninterested, he persisted with the narration of his story.

'It was getting impossible for Lord Ram to leave his body and die as the God of death, Lord Yamraj, had expressed that it would be impossible for him to take Lord Ram's life in the presence of Lord Hanuman, who was an adherent devotee of Lord Ram and would never let him die.'

So, to send Lord Hanuman away, Lord Ram dropped his ring in a fissure on the floor of his palace and told Lord Hanuman to get it.

Lord Hanuman being an adherent devotee, reduced his size and went inside the fissure to search for the ring. However, this fissure went down deep till Nag - Loka, the world of serpents.

On reaching Nag - Loka, Lord Hanuman was initially disheartened to find billions of rings stacked there. Finding a ring in this was akin to finding a needle in a haystack, however, the first ring he picked turned out to be Ram's ring. Later, Lord Hanuman was surprised to find that all the rings in that enormous stack belonged to Lord Ram.

To solve the mystery, Hanuman asked Vasuki, the king of Nag - Loka, about this. King Vasuki said that these rings come down at a fixed time interval in the lifespan of the universe. At a fixed time in Treta Yuga, a monkey comes in search of Ram's ring and every time that monkey comes, Lord Ram dies in the outer world.'

After narrating this story, the hermit gave the paper to Sarvan. 'Keep it! The container may be filthy but the contents are priceless.' After saying that the hermit went away.

Sarvan sat for some time holding the paper in his hand, unaware of what just happened with him, and then he folded the paper and kept it inside his pocket.

Rohan and Santy came back with packed food for the entire gang. Rohan walked with the food in his hand towards the tree under which Sarvanhad been sitting. Shiv was lying in the back of the truck. Rohan's mother and Vani were inside the temple.

'This is for you mate,' Santy said, handing over a packet of packed food to Shiv. 'Sorry about that evil comment. I think you are a pretty chilled out guy when you are not making bullets disappear and people fly.'

Shiv smiled and extended his hand towards Santy. Santy was about to shake his hand when suddenly, as if out of nowhere, an arrow pierced the right temple of Santy's head and came out from the other side.

The lifeless body of Santy fell like a broken log on top of Shiv. At the same moment, a spray of bullets covered the area. Rohan and Sarvan took cover behind the tree under which they were sitting.

Shiv quickly gathered all his energy to stand and created a kind of energy shield which could stop bullets.

An arrow broke through the energy shield and pierced Shiv's shoulder. Shiv cried out in pain and fell to his knees, but he was still able to hold the shield intact preventing the bullets from hurting anyone.

Around thirty to forty men surrounded Shiv and his friends from all sides and unleashed a fury of bullets and shot mysterious arrows.

At a high ground about a hundred meters from Shiv's location, Marich stood along with Aghora and watched the entire scene unfold.

At an appropriate time, Aghora moved ahead holding a stick with a large round crystal on its head. Aghora raised his hand to signal everyone to stop firing and then closed his eyes and raised his stick. Three black shadows appeared out of the crystal head of the stick and sprang together towards Shiv.

The shadows easily crossed the energy shield that Shiv created and started swirling around Shiv. Then, in the nick of a moment, one of the shadows entered into Shiv's left nostril. Shiv shrugged in disgust and all of a sudden, felt weak.

I felt as if my connection with Shiv's brain had suddenly been severed. I felt the space around me closing down as if trying to engulf me. I tried to shift into another brain, of either Sarvan or Rohan but felt as if I was trapped inside Shiv's brain. The claustrophobia was nauseating. And then there was complete darkness and absolute muteness. A dead silence.

CHAPTER 9

THE THIRD EYE COVERUP

I realised that I was still alive when Shiv opened his eyes and I again glimpsed the outside world after what felt like ages.

It was some kind of an enormous glass laboratory and Shiv was bound inside a cylindrical glass container on the top floor of the laboratory.

From where Shiv was standing, I could see at least four floors full of lab beakers of different shapes and sizes, with strange coloured liquids bubbling inside them.

At the centre of the huge office where we were kept was a huge ivory dining table surrounded by white chairs. At the far end of the dining table sat a tall bald man eating something. Two suited and muscular men stood guard behind him. Shiv's Shree - Yantra was kept on the dining table near the bald man.

'Welcome back home, Shiv. My name is Marich Natraj,' the bald man said in a deep husky voice while eating his food.

'You killed Santy, you bastard! Where are my other friends?' Shiv asked.

The bald man stopped eating and looked towards Shiv with a steely stare that could send Shivers down anyone's spine.

'Don't ever use abusive language with me again, Shiv. I get really offended,' Marich said.' those friends of yours were already dead when they decided to steal you from me. However, I am very pleased by the display of your capacity to endure pain and your desire to live. For eighteen years you survived everything that we injected into you, and then you came back rejuvenated.

You even defeated my men with these powers of yours. In the last thirty - one years, I have rarely been surprised by people. But in your case, I must admit, even I was surprised.'

'What did you do with my friends? What are you up to?' Shiv asked again.

'Your friends are now subjects for my experiments; they will meet their fate soon. We had to kill the old lady as she didn't match the physical parameters required to test our drugs. She was useless. But you have proven yourself to be worthy of knowing about the mission that you are a part of. The mission that will change the world forever,' Marich said and pressed a button on a remote that moved the vessel in which Shiv was encaged to the edge of the wall - sized glass window and then turned it around to let Shiv face him.

'Do you know what is the greatest power that mankind has been endowed with, Shiv?' Marich asked.

Shiv remained silent.

'Human world has not been created by knowledge. Knowledge is available in the market, it can be bought. I can hire a person with knowledge to work for me.

Human world is a manifestation of human imagination. Imagination cannot be purchased, it is a human quality. Imagination is the greatest power possessed by mankind.

Humans imagined religions, nations, families, law system, financial system etc. The fact that humans saw sunrise and hypothesised gravitation and the model of the solar system after it, is the power of human imagination. Just think what would happen if I get the power to control human imagination!' Marich said.

'Control human imagination! How is that possible? Imagination cannot be controlled,' Shiv said in disbelief.

'Well, be prepared to get startled, Shiv,' Marich said.' After many years of studying the human brain, scientists discovered a mysterious body part. It was about the size of a pea and remained hidden between both the lobes of the brain. They called it Pineal Gland.

It is a kind of endocrine gland that looks like a small pine and secretes hormones directly into the brain rather than through any medium.

Interestingly, this small gland is also called the Third Eye as it is constructed exactly like an eye. It is filled with water with very tiny crystals floating in it, and in the internal membrane, it has structures similar to rods and cones found in a normal human eye. Moreover, it is connected to the visual cortex of the brain and gets activated by the light and the dark. The only difference it has, is that it is oriented to look upwards towards the brain rather than outside the body.

The common understanding is that it controls the bio - rhythms of a human body. It determines sexual and hunger necessities and regulates the sleep cycle of a human body; it also regulates the ageing process of a human body.

For modern science, this tiny body part remained hidden for centuries, but there are numerous pieces of evidence that ancient civilizations were aware of the secrets of pineal glands. In fact, it has always been the central part of ancient mythologies and mysteries. It has been worshipped to be divine since the time humans came into existence.

In ancient Egypt, it was known as the Eye of Horus or the Eye of Ra. It is considered as a symbol of power, health, and safety and is found to be a central theme in almost all ancient Egyptian artefacts or mummies.

Notice the extreme similarity of the pineal gland with the Eye of Ra.

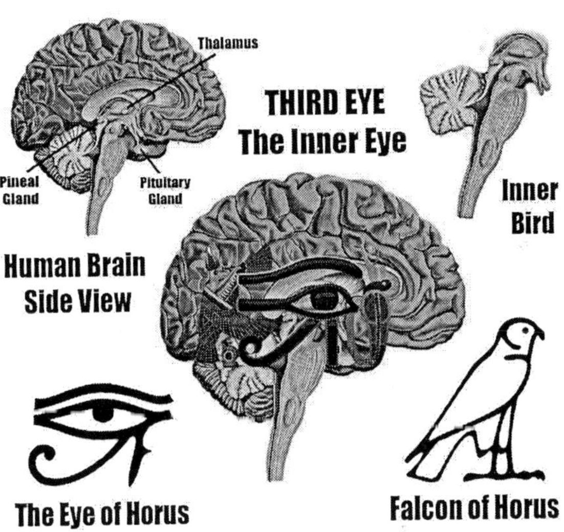

And that is not all. In Buddhism, Lord Gautama Buddha is always depicted with a third eye on his forehead and pine shaped hair on his head which symbolises pineal gland.

Ancient Samarians like the Annu'naki, who are considered among the most scientifically advanced people ever to walk on Earth, have the symbol of this pine or third eye everywhere as a central theme. In Rome, Italy, and the Vatican, the Pope always carries a stick with a symbol of pine on top.

Even today, the forefathers of United States of America added the Illuminati symbol of the all - seeing third eye at the back of a dollar note.

So what was so special about this mysteriously shrouded, tiny pine - shaped part deeply hidden inside our brains that accorded it an almost God - like reverence among almost all ancient civilisations and religions?

Very recently, after years of research, we have been able to decipher some of its secrets.

Modern advancements in science led to a strange discovery that the study of the human brain is not entirely a subject of biology; it is, in fact, more of a subject of chemistry.

Your emotions, moods, feelings, happiness, sadness, dreams, and intuitions are not just arbitrary creations or reactions of your brain. They are the results of specific quantities of neurotransmitter hormones secreted by the pineal gland. And I am not talking only about these emotions; even the greatest powers of mind are a chemical reaction of these hormones.

It is the connecting link between the physical and the spiritual world. It is like a cosmic antenna created to receive signals from God. Due to the vital role played by this gland in the manifestation of life, it is also called 'the Seed of Soul'.

It secretes several hormones and two commonly known ones are called Serotonin and Melatonin.

In the morning, when the sun's intensity is higher, serotonin is secreted. It controls your mood swings. If there is a deficiency of serotonin in your body, it will make one very depressed and stressful. However, if it is present in excess in your brain, then also it can lead to sickness and even to insanity. But, serotonin in just the right quantity is responsible for making you happy and balanced.

However, that is not all. During our research, we tested the effects of serotonin on some weak or let's call them beta males and the results showed that with just the right amount of serotonin, they turned to alpha males with increased physical strength, sexual appetite, and aggressiveness.

For a normal human being, there are certain actions which lead to the release of serotonin, like winning a lottery or scoring good in an exam which makes one feel good or happy. But the issue was, what determines this optimum level of serotonin?

Let me explain it like this, that, when a person takes drugs, he artificially injects himself with neurotransmitter hormones like serotonin. He raises the datum for the measure of happiness. So the next time when that person will win a lottery, the serotonin level will increase but will fall short of the level required to make him feel happy. So the next time, he can feel happiness only when the same quantity of serotonin is released by the pineal gland. But that will not be possible by doing any action; the only way to do it is by taking more drugs. This way that person becomes addicted to drugs.

At night, when the light levels are low, another hormone called melatonin gets secreted. Technically, this hormone works like a coolant and ensures that the brain doesn't overwork itself to death by inducing and regulating the sleep cycle. If one sleeps for the correct amount and the correct quantity, melanin is released which also increases your lifespan. It may sound strange but melatonin reduces bone loss and it also ensures bone flexibility and strength.

Similarly, all your emotions connected with love and anger are connected with another hormone called Dopamine.

But the most astonishing discovery had been made most recently in the form of Dimethyltryptamine (DMT). According to work done by Dr. Rick Strassman, it is a psychedelic drug produced naturally by the pineal gland and he named it 'the Spirit Molecule' because of its 'Godly' properties.

Now, DMT is present in every living being, be it plants or animals. It is a universally prominent chemical in all life forms but till now, no one had ever been able to determine its significance. No one had been able to answer what exactly does it do?

The conventional wisdom about it was that it has no real function and it is just present as some form of physiological aberration.

Our initial experiments on plants revealed that plants use DMT as their language of communication. That was a phenomenal finding and it prompted us to continue our research until we discovered that DMT is a kind of messenger molecule which plants use as they are in a perpetual state of meditation. In a deep state of meditation, the release of DMT by the pineal gland allows plants to communicate with all other species of nature in a similar meditative state.

Since plants and animals have grown together, we extended our researches to animals and finally, to humans.

There is a molecular language by which all living beings on this planet communicate. What we have termed to behuman feelingsare generated by this molecule only. This is the hormone that connects you to your Consciousness and further, to Universal Consciousness.

In humans, DMT gives a kind of spiritual or out - of - body

experience. Some illegal drugs in the market are based on compounds similar in construction to DMT. For example, there is a drug named LSD which utilizes a similar chemical composition as DMT. One intake of such a drug will give a person an out - of - body experience in which they are not limited by their physical self.

Under the influence of DMT, almost all the subjects reported encountering angels and higher beings or experiencing higher realms of life detached from the present world. The problem occurs when they revert back to normalcy. They find it difficult to associate themselves with their normal limited selves and want to have the same experiences again and again. Human life appears to them as a burden. That's why many drug addicts outcast themselves from social life and some even commit suicide.

In the human body, the release of DMT is completely controlled by the pineal gland and that makes it the most important part of the human body for psychics, religious figures, and anyone else into meditative practices.

If developed through the power of meditation, the gland slowly prepares the brain for supernatural experiences by releasing controlled quantities of DMT till the mind is ready. It has the power to make a human brain break out of reality and achieve superhuman feats. One can use this gland to achieve money, success, or even love.

Modern scientists have called this gland'the Seat of the Soul' because this is the connecting point between the mind and the body. This is the gateway to your own cosmic self or the universe.

Tibetan Book of the Dead states that 49 days after death, a soul is reincarnated. A human embryo can be distinguished from male to female on the 49th day of conceiving. As per Hinduism, a soul enters a body on the 49th day and it may be more than a coincidence that the pineal gland appears in the human body on the 49th day and releases its first dose of DMT.

Pineal Gland secretes DMT under conditions of extreme

stress. Many people encountering near - death situations have talked about spiritual or outer body visualisations, triggered by moments of intense stress. There are examples of scientists and inventors receiving knowledge during a period of extreme stress or deep sleep, or of mothers getting intuitions about their kids even when they are far from them.

In some cases, even music has the capability to influence the pineal gland to secrete DMT as experienced by trans - music or used by some chains of yoga gurus to bring their disciples in a joyous state.

But the most common and the best method of releasing DMT is through deep meditation as it slowly conditions your brain for the visualisation that one is about to receive and gradually uplifts the person to higher levels by raising the datum.

The pineal gland is the source of all human powers that we know or don't know about. If a human being realises his potential, he can cure himself, live as long as he desires, dream, invent new things; in fact, he can accomplish everything that is possible with human imagination.

But what if we have some way of curbing this human imagination?' Marich said, with a wicked smile to Shiv.

'How can anyone stop human imagination?' Shiv asked.

'Simply by destroying the source of these hormones in the human body,' Marich said and continued, there are neurotoxins that can be used to attack and destroy the pineal gland. The worst enemy of the pineal gland are Halides, which are chemical substances like fluoride, chloride, and bromide.

Did you know that in Nazi concentration camps, the prisoners were given very large quantities of fluoridated water to keep them docile and pacified and to destroy their resistance capability?

Fluoride, in particular, is like poison for the pineal gland. Fluoride leads to the formation of calcium phosphate crystals on the pineal gland by a process known as Calcification of the Pineal Gland also referred to as Brain Sand. This leads to many other diseases in human beings known as Parkinson's, Alzheimer, Cancer, and Autism', Marich said.

'I don't understand. What will you guys gain by destroying such a vital component of the human body?' Shiv asked.

'We destroy! Oh no, Shiv, we don't destroy people's pineal glands. That job is done by the Governments of different countries. We bribe them and they allow the consumption of our products in their countries.

This fluoride can be fed to the society on a large scale by a variety of sources like fluoride toothpastes, fluoridated water, soft drinks, artificial sweeteners, and even excessive usage of cell phones.

There are other sources of ingesting halides into the human body like processed food, preservatives, mercury filling in teeth, and even some vaccines. Non - vegetarian food, in particular, contains a high amount of calcium and that is why people practising deep meditation are advised to eat vegetarian food.

As per a report, around 40% people in the United States of America alone have their pineal glands calcified up to 50% by the time they reach the age of seventeen.

You see, the increase in diseases like cancer, impotency, and mental illness in modern society is a result of this. It has been going on for a long time and has been very well - executed. We merely make use of the foundation created by smart men before us,' Marich said.

'How will creating a weak and unimaginative society serve your interests? Is it about money?' Shiv asked.

'Money! Do you think I bother about money? Shiv, this is for a bigger cause. See, we have been working upon a mission. We increased the fluoride dosage in drinking water and pesticides to hasten the calcification of the pineal gland of the society.

Only a selected few elite classes will be protected against this. We have already reached near the termination of this phase. Your friend's impotency, Rohan's father's cancer, and your autism were side effects of this mission only. Once the pineal gland becomes ineffective, the brain becomes vulnerable.

The second phase of our mission is just about to begin. Recently, my devoted team of scientists were able to create a serum through which we can artificially inject the necessary chemicals in the human body. This will cause their brains to get manipulated simply by means of certain vibrations.

Once we are able to do that, we will create an entire army of devoted slaves who will act as per our desires. We will be able to manipulate their brains by triggering certain frequencies.

Think about it, Shiv. Think about workers who have no desires, no sexual interests, and no sadness. They will willingly accept me as their master and work throughout their life for me. Human imagination makes them question things, it makes them insubordinate; once we remove the element of human imagination from them, they will just be a bunch of devoted workers with no other desire but to serve me. It will be a perfect cure.' Marich was speaking like a possessed devil.

'You want to turn normal human beings into robots so that you can rule over them. You want to destroy the complete system of society. For God's sake, these are living souls,' Shiv rebelled.

'Are they living? Shiv, the world has forever been divided into masters and servants. Even today, there are only a few elite who invent things or control the entire business and the governments of the world, the balance majority of humanity is just crowd.

They take birth, work for the elite, and die. They live a pathetic life and die a miserable death and throughout their life, they shun their imagination to work for their masters.

The society you are talking about never used their power of imagination anyway; they were born followers who followed the norms that I made for them to follow.

When the elite class needed managers, they all studied MBA; when they needed engineers, they all did engineering. They were never individuals, they were mass followers. They only studied to become slaves to some elite human.

The world has forever been enjoyed by only a few. All luxuries and everything desirable has been made by keeping the interests of these elite alpha men in mind.

Humans have themselves chosen to live like slaves instead of exploring their potential. I am just providing them with a higher purpose to serve. Humans want to serve a God, so here I am, ready to enslave them. They can serve me without distraction.

Shiv, your concerns for this slave race are unfounded. I am just making them more obedient and removing their miseries. They get a regular dose of the serum and remain happy workers. And then one day, we will have to enact the third phase which we call 'The Final Solution'. Marich appeared more sinister than what he was sounding till now.

'What could be worse than a lifeless soulless generation of mankind?' Shiv asked.

'This is to preserve Mother Nature. We have learnt that if you drop the hormonal level below a datum, a person commits suicide. The final solution is to inject worthless workers with serums that will reduce their depression level to the extent that they will be driven to commit mass suicides. Today, we have the testing of this serum. We have already injected the subjects,' Marich said and clapped thrice.

The huge office door opened and three shadows walked in. In an instant, Shiv recognised the three subjects.

'No...not them...Rohan, Sarvan, and Vani...please, these are my friends. If you want to test the serum, you can do it on me. I am your lab subject, not them,' Shiv cried at the top of his voice.

'Relax, Shiv, the ones you are calling friends are just insects of the society. They have to be cleaned anyways. Besides, it is too late now. They have already been injected with our latest serum. These minor sacrifices must never matter in the pursuit of bigger goals. You of all people must know that Shiv,' Marich said and stared at Shiv.

Shiv stood staring at Marich to decode the mysterious look that Marich was giving.

Marich smiled for the first time, came close to Shiv and said, 'You don't remember anything, do you? You really don't know why you are alive or why am I spending my time giving you all these details? Well, it may be because you were very young at that time.'

'What do you know about my childhood?' Shiv asked in disbelief.

'I know everything,' Marich said in a cold tone, after all, '*I AM YOUR FATHER*'.

CHAPTER 10

GHOSTS OF THE PAST

It was as if lightning had struck Shiv by the last disclosure made by Marich.' You are what?' Shiv shouted.

'Of course, it is expected, how would you know? But the truth is I am your father,' Marich said. 'I am a businessman and my business requires a continuous supply of human test subjects like you. When you ran away from me, I could have got you killed but I searched for you because you are special to me Shiv.

You are no match for the psychic powers of Aghora but I restrained him. Do you know I had to get special arrows made of Rudraksh to pierce through your energy field?

Of all the materials found in nature, rudraksh has the most unique composition that creates the most unique energy shield around it. Depending on the type of work required to be extracted, a suitable rudraksh with an appropriate number of faces is required. For you, Shiv, we chose Ekamukhior a single - faced rudraksh. Those arrows that pierced through your energy field could have also pierced your heart. Why do you think I have kept you alive, Shiv? I will tell you the reason. You are dear to me. And so was your mother,' Marich said.

Tears started rolling down Shiv's eyes.' You devil! For twenty - four years you have made me live like a dead corpse.' Shiv's eyes were turning red with anger, his body was shaking.' And today you have come to claim me.'

As the conversation between Shiv and Marich began to get intense, something strangely familiar was happening inside Shiv's brain. I could see a mild red glow over Shiv's brain getting darker and slowly taking a shape. I had witnessed this sight below. It was Ego.

The more the ego grew, the more I was separated from Shiv's brain.

Ego grew in size and my hold on Shiv's brain became weaker. I was desperate for Shiv's attention. Ego was overpowering me and I was losing my complete control over Shiv's brain.

'Shiv! Shiv!' I tried to communicate with him but the fit of rage had filled his brain with ego.

Vani and Rohan had a zombie look in their eyes and apparently, they were completely unaware of the loud conversation between Shiv and Marich. Both of them were acting differently. Vani was trembling as if she was possessed by a demon; Rohan was unnaturally quiet; only Sarvan seemed to have some semblance of life left in his body. His body was still trying to resist the effects of the drug that had been injected into it.

'There are situations which you won't understand, Shiv. Well, one day, I will tell you about your mother. I really liked her,' Marich said.

'What I understand is that you are a monster who is conspiring to finish human life by controlling human minds after destroying their pineal glands. And whatever you say won't stop me from destroying you.' Shiv was fuming with rage.

Marich paused for a while and said with a grim look on his face, 'I do not like that tone, Shiv. You are much like your mother.' Marich moved to a side and grabbed Vani by her hair and pulled her close to himself.

'I want you in this project with me, Shiv, and I don't take no for an answer.' Marich took out a small knife from his pocket. 'I will cut this pretty face if it is needed to make your decision - making easier.'

'Leave her!' Shiv cried, 'I swear Marich I will kill you if you touch her.'

Marich lifted his hand to place the knife on the throat of the bemused Vani. Suddenly, out of nowhere, Rohan came running and banged his head on Marich's back.

The impact was sudden and massive and sent the huge body of Marich thrown to a side. Vani fainted and fell on the spot. The bodyguards of Marich came into action and leaped to catch hold of Rohan who was now running around the room like a wild bull.

Marich got up furiously. He was agitated and swung his fist into the face of the charging Rohan. In a single blow, Rohan was knocked unconscious on the ground.

With Vani and Rohan unconscious and Shiv's anger making him unreceptive of me, Sarvan was the only option left for me. If I could get into the mind of Sarvan, I could probably do something.

But only Shiv could teleport me into the brains of my other connections and with every passing second, Ego was getting fuelled and I was losing my hold.

Marich was madly driven by rage. He got up and came to Shiv holding the knife in his hand.

'Maybe I was mistaken. It was a bad idea. I should have known. You have her DNA. I should have killed you along with your mother.' With those words, Marich swung the knife and made a clean cut across the artery in Shiv's neck.

The shock of life fading away with every breath had suddenly reduced ego to oblivion and I could feel every single emotion that was playing in Shiv's mind.

Shiv was dying. We were about to lose the most important war against evil.

Then the picture started shaking. In his last dying moments, with blood oozing out of his neck and his breath fading away, Shiv was still trying to concentrate to do something.

Then, in a snap moment, the picture in front of me changed and I could now see the dead body of Shiv lying in a pool of blood. I was watching him lying dead from Sarvan's eyes.

Before dying, Shiv had made his final move. He had teleported me into Sarvan.

CHAPTER 11

PARALLEL UNIVERSES

Sarvan's brain felt different. There was no trace of self - pity or depression that had characterised Rohan ever since I had known him.

The drugs that had been injected into Sarvan had sent him into a trance. Normal human brains function within certain bandwidth just like all other human organs. However, under the influence of drugs, the brain loses control and ventures into dimensions incomprehensible to humans. That is why they see colours and have an out - worldly experience that makes them an addict and ruins their lives.

For the first time, Sarvan's mind was out of the extents defined by Sarvan's brain. For Sarvan, it meant total unfathomable disconnect with the events happening around and non - control over his Indriyans. But for me, it meant freedom.

I looked around to find Chit or whosoever could help me.

But except for my own bluish glow, it was all darkness around. I could see Marich shouting furiously at his bodyguards. I suspected it was not long before he loses control again in a fit of rage and harms Sarvan, Vani or Rohan.

'How can there be so many rings?' A sound echoed in Sarvan's brain.

For a moment I was astounded. 'Sarvan! Can you hear me?' I asked.

'How can there be so many rings?' Sarvan asked again.

Maybe he was hallucinating about something. Despite my best efforts, I could not communicate with Sarvan. At last, I gave up the efforts.

At a distance I could see a few people wearing lab coats entering Marich's office with some medical equipment's and inserting some needles in Vani and Rohan's body.

Even if they were inserting something in Sarvan's body, I could not feel anything because I was disconnected with his Indriyans. I had never felt so helpless and so meaningless in the duration of my entire existence.

And then, as if out of nowhere, it struck me. 'How can there be so many rings?'

Sarvan's subconscious mind was stuck at a very logical point of contention in the story he had heard very recently. The mythological story where Lord Ram sends Lord Hanuman to get his ring from Nag - Loka and when Lord Hanuman reaches there, he finds a whole mountain of rings wherein every single ring belonged to Lord Ram. When asked, King Vasuki told Lord Hanuman that every time such a ring falls down, a monkey comes looking for it.

This story clearly talks about the infinite times a universe takes birth and collapses. Everytime a new universe is born, the cycles of the four Yugas get repeated. So we will have Satyuga, Tretayuga, Dwaparyuga, and Kaliyuga being repeated several times in one life time of the universe.

Whenever Treta Yuga will be ongoing in the lifetime of the Universe, Lord Ram will take birth and the events of his lifetime will get repeated.

This story is in perfect sync with the modern scientific theory wherein a universe gets created by an event called 'The Big Bang' in which a universe expands till it reaches its maximum expanse after which starts the phase of 'The Big Crunch' wherein the universe contracts and so on the cycle continues.

But there was a catch in the story which Sarvan's thinking mind had caught.

If the event of Ram's ring falling in Nag - loka happened infinite times, then the event of Lord Hanuman taking the ring back to Lord Ram also took place infinite times as a subsequent event every single time.

So, if every time Lord Hanuman took back the ring, then there should not be any ring left. Also, once the universe lives its life then the ring must also get destroyed along with the universe. So in either case, there should be only one ring that Lord Hanuman should find.

So, *how can there be so many rings*? In a single timeline, even if an event happens multiple number of times, at one point of time it will happen only once. There is absolutely no explanation of why an infinite number of rings should be present at a place at a single point of time.

There was no rational explanation except one. For a moment, I could not believe my own conclusion.

The probability of thousands of rings present at one point of time is possible only if the event is not going on in a single timeframe. If there are multiple time frames and the same event is going on in all the time frames simultaneously,only then it is possible that all the rings will be collected in Nag - Loka at the same time. The simple story told by the hermit had a deep hidden meaning. It explained the multiverse or the parallel universe theory. To understand it, let me explain what dimensions are.

A dimension is nothing but a direction perpendicular to the previous direction.

Let us consider a single dot. This dot has neither length nor breadth nor height. In short, it can be said to be having zero dimensions.

A One - Dimensional being is someone who can travel from one dot to infinite other dots along any one direction or a single line. So, a single line can be said to have only one dimension i. e. length. Let us term this particular direction along the length as x axis.

A Two - Dimensional being would be someone who can travel from one line to infinite other lines in any one direction. Since extending that line means moving along the same line, hence, there is only one way one can move from one line to infinite other lines. And that is if one moves perpendicular to it along a plane. So, this being can move along the length and breadth or what we call to bex axis and y axis respectively.

A Third - Dimensional being would be someone who can travel from one plane to infinite other planes in a direction. If we assume one paper to be a plane, then a third - dimensional being can move along a stack of papers kept one above the other in a vertical direction. So, this being would have length, breadth and height or 'x,' 'y' and 'z' axis.

Now, to understand the fourth - dimension, let us assume a cube as a three - dimensional being. By applying the same analogy as before, a Fourth - Dimensional being should be able to move from one cube to infinite other cubes in any one direction. Whereas, the world we perceive appears to be static within its space. Actually, what we fail to notice is that we also move ahead in time.

Time as the Fourth - Dimension can be perceived in two ways.

Either we can have a single cube which is moving ahead in time in which case time will be 'time' as we know it.

But we can also see fourth - dimension as a continuous series of cubes kept adjoined with each other, with each cube representing an instant. So life, as we know it, plays like a movie tape in which every instant has been captured on a film and at any one instant, only one film is projected. However, when the complete film is played, everything appears to be in motion.

If we see time in this particular manner, it can be called as space. Hence, the words time and space are spoken together. A fourth - dimensional being is someone who can go back and forth in time.

If time is the fourth - dimension, then what could define the fifth - dimension?

As discussed earlier, dimension is nothing but a direction perpendicular to the plane that is being considered. The only thing that can move perpendicular to the plane of time is decision. Let me explain this with the example of human life.

Let us say, a child studies biology and grows up to become a doctor. This is the timeline of his life. In other words, this is the line his life will follow for a set of decisions that he takes in his lifetime. But what if he had taken the decision of studying engineering instead of medicine at some point in his lifetime?

In that case, his timeline would have been different. He might have become an engineer and followed a completely different course of life. In other words, he would have followed a timeline perpendicular to the original timeline.

Likewise, any man in his lifetime takes thousands of decisions to follow a certain timeline. However, if one could go back in time and change any one decision, he would realise that his timeline would completely change. He would experience a different future. He would experience a completely different universe. This is what is called 'Parallel Universe'. This is the Fifth - Dimension.

A person in the fifth - dimension can go back in time and change a decision he had made to enter a parallel universe whose future would be different in accordance with the new decision that has been made.

There are these moments in everyone's life when one makes life - changing decisions. In such moments, a person must listen to Me, his Consciousness, because only I have the power to transcend dimensions and understand what is best for that person.

To understand the sixth - dimension, we can consider a plane comprising the fourth and fifth - dimension.

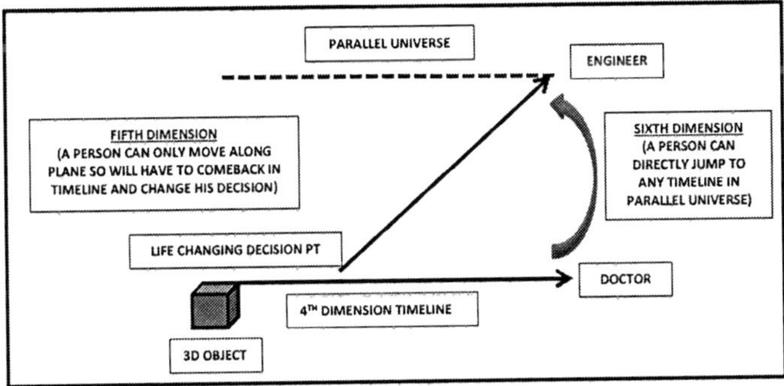

Imagine it like a paper on which time is represented in the form of a line and an alternate decision is just a branch protruding perpendicular to that timeline on the plane of that paper.

Since the fifth - dimension has been represented as the plane of that paper, if a person in the fifth - dimension wants to change his timeline, he would have to travel back to the point where he took a life - changing decision along his timeline and then, take the alternate decision at that precise point. That means he would have to get young again, take the alternate decision, and re - live the complete lifetime as a result of that decision.

A person sitting in the sixth - dimension is someone located in the plane perpendicular to the plane of the paper which comprises time and decision. He will have the ability to jump from any point in this timeline to the other timeline by utilising the perpendicular dimension or the sixth - dimension.

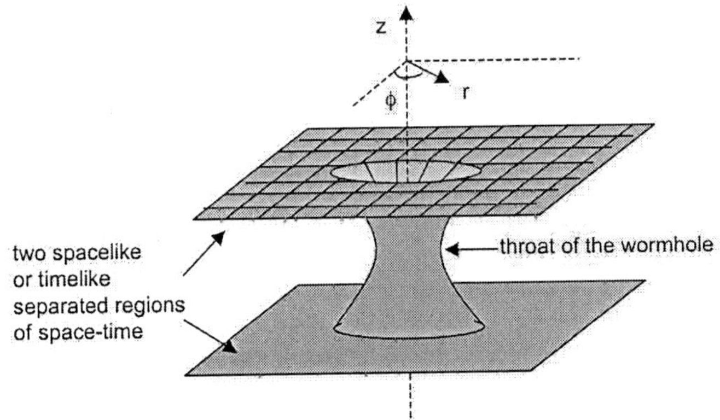

So, if we consider the fourth - dimension as x - axis and the fifth - dimension as the y - axis, then the sixth - dimension can be considered along the z - axis. Sixth Dimension can be understood in the form of a wormhole on the universal plane connecting Parallel Universes.

These dimensions are not divided by distances; they are, in fact, coexisting at any given point but are inaccessible due to the incapability of the form of creation.

If we consider a stack of papers, the words written on one page cannot cross over to the page kept on top of it despite the fact that the papers are exactly touching each other. The reason is that written words are two - dimensional and cannot travel in a vertical direction.

The story of Ram's ring pulsating in Sarvan's semi - conscious mind was stuck at this simple logical protuberance.

For any human being, it is impossible to travel back in time as his physical body is three - dimensional. But for me, travelling to different dimensions was just a part of self - discovery.

I saw a ray of hope. I came up with a plan which could get everyone out of the clutches of Marich.

My plan was simple. If I could go back in time and change any one life - changing decision, then we would experience a completely new present. A new present that might turn the fortunes in favour of us. The question was which could be this life - changing decision.

I mean, I had to go back to a time when Santy and Rohan's mother were alive, but when?

My dilemma was solved by Sarvan's brain in the simplest possible manner. The sober erstwhile software engineer had been through the most adventurous day of his life. The impact of shock, coupled with the effect of drugs had been so overwhelming on Sarvan's mind, that ithad temporarily erased most of his memories except todays.

At a distance, Marich was standing with a grim face and a man in a white labcoat had removed the needles from Rohan's arm.

'The results are better than we expected,' said the man in the white coat. 'I think we are ready.'

Marich forced a devilish smile on his face. 'It is time to move to the next level. Let me remove traces of these distractions from my sight first. Without Shiv, they serve no useful purpose for me now,' Marich said and moved towards Sarvan with his blood stained knife.

Sarvan's mind was wandering in unknown dimensions and it was impossible for me to get him to concentrate to send me to any chosen point in the timeline. In a few seconds, Marich would rip off life from Sarvan's body. I took the most prominent memory in Sarvan's mind.

In the limited time available to make my choice, I had made my First Life - Changing Decision.

CHAPTER 12

THE LIFE - CHANGING DECISION

I woke up in the surroundings of an ancient temple under a banyan tree looking at a hermit standing in front of me.

'If you take it from me, I will also tell you a story of Lord Ram,' the hermit insisted.

'Why? I don't want to hear any story. Please leave me alone,' Sarvan tried to shrug him aside.

I instantly connected to the turn of events happening here. The last memory in Sarvan's mind was of this hermit trying to sell him a story. I had been teleported back into time to a point where the attack by Marich's militia was about to happen.

'Sarvan…you got to run from here. Collect everybody.' I told Sarvan to look around to find the rest of the family members.

'It is Lord Ram's story, every story of Lord Ram is incredible,' the hermit persisted.

'Leave it, baba,' Sarvan said and quickly moved to find the rest of the people.' Guys…listen, everyone…we got to move from here…I have got a very bad feeling about this place…where is Vani?'Sarvan was breathless as he ran to collect all the family members.

'But we have come quite far from Goa, I don't think they can find us here,' said Santy, while holding a bag of packed breakfast.

'Santy! You fat bastard!' Sarvan said and ran to kiss Santy on his cheek. Santy gave a mixture of surprised and disgusted look.

'Shiv, just don't ask any questions. Collect everyone, we got to move. I will just get Vani,' Sarvan said and ran inside the temple.

The temple belonged to Lord Padmanabha. Among many other sculptures, the central idol had Lord Vishnu sleeping on a coiled serpent floating on an ocean and a lotus coming out of the navel of Lord Vishnu with Lord Brahma sitting on the lotus. There was also Goddess Laxmi sitting and pressing the feet of Lord Vishnu.

'Is this the God people pay their obeisance to? But it is just an idol,' I thought.

Vani was sitting right in front of the idol and was a little shocked to see Sarvan, but noticing the panic in Sarvan's voice, she followed him outside.

By the time Sarvan moved out, Shiv had already gathered everyone else. They all sat inside the monster truck. Rohan,who was going to drive the truck, turned the ignition.

There was no response in the vehicle.

Rohan twisted the key again and again but could not fill life in the engines of the truck.

'Let me just open the bonnet and check,' Shiv said and moved out from the co - driver's seat.

Suddenly, a bullet sound screamed in the peaceful surrounding and pierced a blood blot out of Shiv's head. A lifeless body of Shiv fell on the truck's bonnet.

I was shell shocked. My best efforts had led to nothing. I suddenly realised that since I was in Sarvan's timeline, everyone else's fate could change except Sarvan's.

With Shiv dead, there was absolutely no protection left for the family. The timespan of the lives of the family members was just a matter of a few minutes. We were sure to be captured again.

Suddenly, I realised that there was another severe blunder that I had made. If the timeline of events remains the same, then

Marich will capture Sarvan, Vani, and Rohan to test his drugs and the only way of coming back to the past again would be if Sarvan remembers exactly the same events that he did under the influence of the drugs. But this time that cannot happen.

In the urgency of moving the family members to a safe location, I had forgotten to allow Sarvan to listen to the hermit's story about Lord Ram. If Sarvan doesn't know that story, then he will not remember it and if he doesn't remember that line, then I will not be able to come back.

I had to search for that hermit. Before getting captured, I needed to hear that story from him.

The timid Mumbai engineer did his battle inoculation as he crawled under the spray of the enemy's bullets and hid behind the tree where the hermit had approached him.

To my delight, the hermit was also hiding behind the same banyan tree.

'Quick, ask the hermit to tell you Lord Ram's story,' I told Sarvan.

'What? Why the hell would I want to hear a goddamn story? I am about to get killed,' Sarvan replied.

The argumentative human being has a tendency to adamantly resist my advice at junctures where it matters most to them.

'Just ask the hermit to tell you the story,' I said again, sternly this time.

Sarvan obeyed this time. 'Excuse me, Sadhuji. Please don't mind me asking you. In fact, I find it strange to even ask you, in fact, even you may find it odd, but can you please tell me the story of Lord Ram that you wanted to tell me and I didn't want to hear?'

I had never heard a more obnoxiously created sentence with the most irritating politeness delivered at the most inappropriate time.

The hermit looked at Sarvan in disbelief, and then, as if contemplating the last desire of a dying man said, 'It is good that you decided to remember Lord Ram at the time of your death. Even by remembering the name of Lord Ram, one can attain salvation.'

Amidst the pandemonium all around, the hermit told the story about Ram's ring again to Sarvan.

Marich was visibly offended that his sniper had mistakenly killed Shiv instead of Santy. He shot the sniper himself.

Except for Vani, all other family members were killed inside the truck. Vani got saved as Rohan had embraced her to shield her from the bullets that ripped his body. Marich later found Sarvan and the hermit hiding behind the tree and took them captive.

The captives were injected with the same drugs. This time I was familiar with the space where Sarvan's mind was wandering. I was able to navigate my way back.

When I opened my eyes I saw a familiar sight.

'If you take it from me, I will also tell you a story of Lord Ram,' a dirty looking hermit, standing in front of me, said.

This time I was facing a dilemma. What is that one life - changing decision that I was supposed to take? How can I affect the future favourably?

My options were very limited. I had to hear the story by the hermit because without that I wouldn't be able to come back. The truck was not going to start, so it was not possible for the family members to run from the place.

Then how do I escape from the gang of Marich?

Moreover, I needed to be inside Sarvan's head to hear Ram's story but to fight Marich, I needed to be inside Shiv's head.

This time the moment hermit finished his story, I took all family members and ran inside the jungle.

But it didn't change things much. Some of Marich's goons were already advancing from the jungle side and were able to capture everyone alive. Shiv was able to fight out for some time till a rudraksh arrow pierced his shoulder and Aghora defeated him exactly like the first time. The sequence of the rest of the events remained the same as the first time.

The event kept on repeating thereafter. Every time I tried to apply a different strategy. It began to dawn upon me that Marich had covered all my options. There was just no way to escape from there.

I tried to hide everyone inside the temple, but we were found by Marich's men. I tried to dodge and protect Shiv from the rudraksh arrows but the number of incoming arrows kept on increasing till they were impossible to dodge. I tried to fight Aghora by predicting his moves to Shiv but with the present powers, it was difficult for Shiv to fight Aghora. I even tried to shift into Rohan's mind but to no avail.

I tried and tried innumerable times as if I was caught in some kind of a vicious loop of time, living the same moment again and again. I was beginning to lose hope. Sometimes, the biggest turn arounds in life come from the smallest and seemingly inconsequential decisions that a human being takes.

Even after living the same moment hundreds of times in a sequence and trying all possible decisions, it was difficult for me to visualise that the 'Life - Changing Decision' I was searching in this time loop, would rest in something so trivial; but then I learnt the truth.

The truth that no matter how big a problem a human being seems to be in, if he is with the side of the truth, then there is a power called God who will always help him. Problems onlyarise when human beings willingly refuse to seek the help of God. The hermit had not turned up by accident; he was there by a precise coincidence to serve a bigger purpose, to unravel more secrets to us.

I had gotten so involved in listening to the story by the hermit that I had almost completely forgotten about the product that he was trying to sell me. I realised my folly when I decided to open and read what was written inside that crumbled piece of paper that the hermit was repeatedly trying to sell me.

'If you take it from me, I will also tell you a story of Lord Ram,' A dirty looking hermit, standing in front of me, said.

'What are you selling me, baba?'Sarvan asked this time.

'It is called Golak Chart. It will help you,' said the hermit and extended a crumbled piece of paper in which he had just eaten *chana* and was now trying to sell to me.

What I had failed to grasp was the reason due to which the hermit was trying to sell this to me? He could very well have asked me 100 Rupees without giving anything in return, but he repeatedly insisted on me having the paper.

The Golak Chart is a pictorial representation of the universe explained in Srimad Bhagavatam and is published by the ISKON society in India.

The explanation of the universe was so fantastic in the chart that it was unbelievably weird. The chart explained the Universe as per God. For simplicity of explanation, I will call it God's Universe.

If I put it briefly, there is a Gods Universe which is divided into three levels. The lowest level is the mundane world which is the abode of Lord Brahma. Above that is the abode of Lord Shiva and at the highest level is the abode of Lord Vishnu. Our ordinary universe lies in the abode of Lord Brahma.

The description of our ordinary universe was even weirder. At the bottom of the chart was a picture similar to the idol inside the temple. It was Lord Vishnu lying on a coiled serpent floating on an ocean. From the navel of Lord Vishnu, a lotus was coming out on top of which Lord Brahma was sitting. But here, in between Vishnu and Brahma, there were 14 Lokas or 14 worlds which were placed.

As per the chart, if we consider our ordinary universe in the form of an egg and name it Brahmanda (Brahma+anda = Egg of Lord Brahma), then it is surrounded by a seven - walled eggshell.

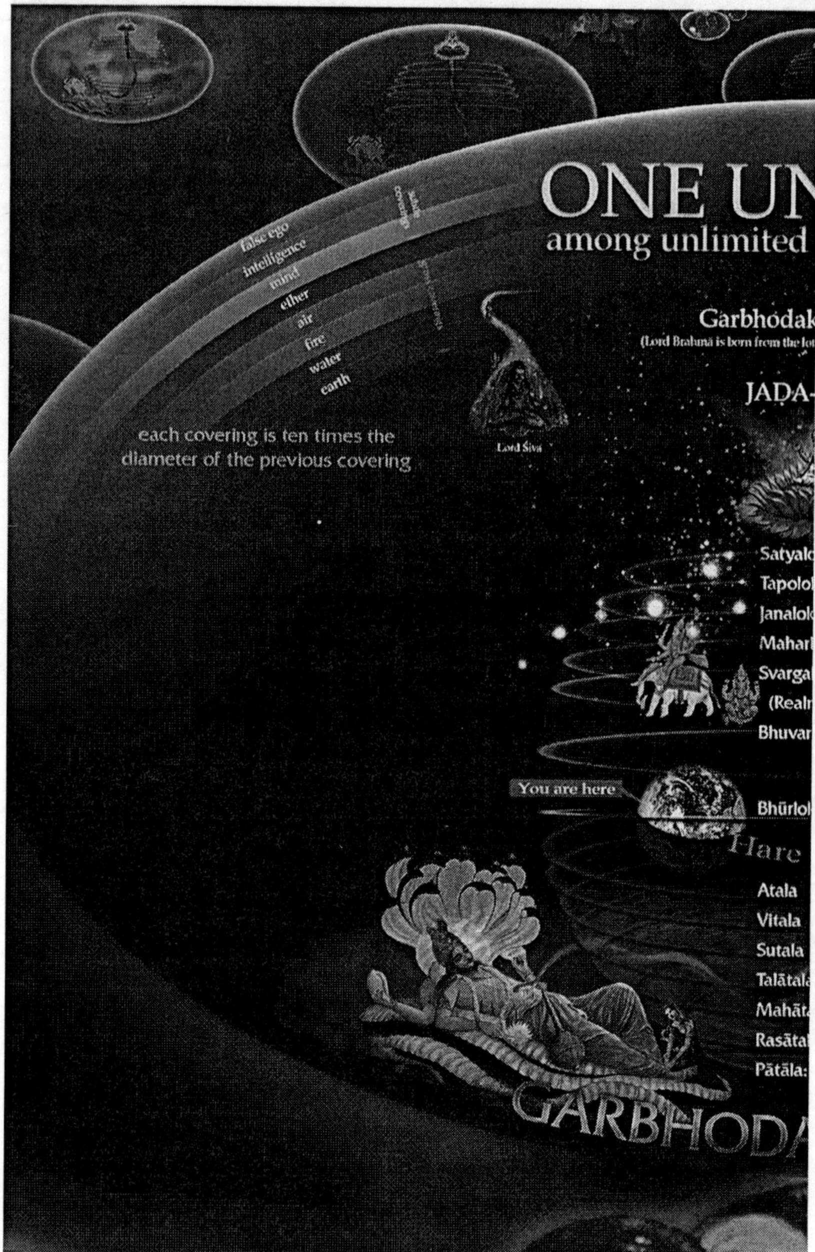
ONE UN
among unlimited
false ego
intelligence
mind
ether
air
fire
water
earth
each covering is ten times the
diameter of the previous covering
Lord Śiva
Garbhodak
JADA-
Satyalo
Tapolo
Janalo
Mahar
Svarga
(Realn
Bhuvar
You are here
Bhūrlo
Hare
Atala
Vitala
Sutala
Talātal
Mahāt
Rasātal
Pātāla:
GARBHODA

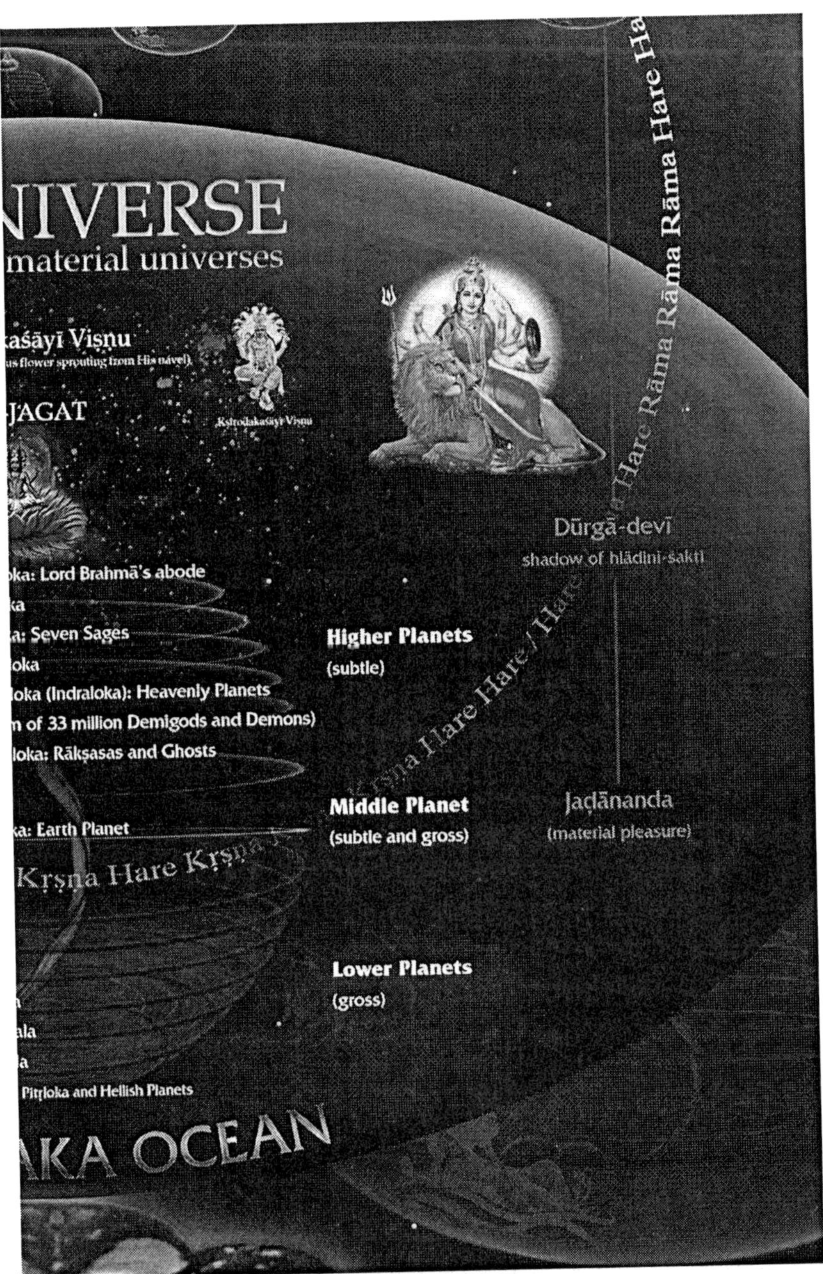
NIVERSE
material universes
aśāyī Viṣṇu
JAGAT
Kṣīrodakaśāyī Viṣṇu
Dūrgā-devī
shadow of hlādini-śakti
ka: Lord Brahmā's abode
a: Seven Sages
oka
loka (Indraloka): Heavenly Planets
n of 33 million Demigods and Demons)
loka: Rākṣasas and Ghosts
a: Earth Planet
Higher Planets
(subtle)
Middle Planet
(subtle and gross)
Jaḍānanda
(material pleasure)
Lower Planets
(gross)
Pitṛloka and Hellish Planets
AKA OCEAN
Kṛṣṇa Hare Kṛṣṇa
Kṛṣṇa Hare Hare / Hare Hare Rāma Rāma Rāma Hare Hare

The seven shells, from inner to outer layers, comprise Earth, water, fire, air, ether, ego, and maha - tattva (some kind of supernatural celestial element). Within this eggshell lay the 14 worlds which comprise our ordinary universe. The description of these 14 worlds (Lokas) is as follows:

- Satyaloka – This is the abode of Lord Brahma and the highest level that can be reached within our ordinary universe. It is the realm where a person finds Moksha. Here, the Supreme Consciousness exists in its infinite form.
- Tapoloka – This is the abode of four super - intelligent five - year - old kids called 'Kumars' namely Sanat, Sanak, Sanandan, and Sanatan. They are considered to be the first reincarnations of Lord Vishnu and personification of all knowledge. It is the realm of psychic energies and ascetics.
- Janaloka – This is the abode of Prajapatis or the realm of the liberated Immortals. They can travel to any part of the world in a blink.
- Maharloka–This is the abode of great sages and rishis. They have a life span nearly equal to the life span of the universe.
- Swargloka – This is the abode of 33 different demigods. It is the kingdom of Lord Indra and all the demi - gods live in opulence here.
- Bhuvarloka – This is the region between Earth and the Sun or what the astronauts have termed to be Space. This is the realm of spirits or when souls are transcending from Earth to higher levels. These souls and spirits may also influence human life sometimes.
- Bhurloka – This is the Earth or the realm of Mortal human beings where we all reside. This world lies exactly in the centre of the 14 worlds.

Below these upper worlds which constitute the higher realms, the chart also mentioned seven lower realms or seven lower worlds namely Atala, Vitala, Sutala, Talatala, Mahatala, Rasatals, and Patala. These realms are inhabited by demons and Rakshas but they live in even more opulence than the beings of Swarg Loka.

The difference between upper and lower worlds was that at higher levels, the metaphysical beings were more spiritually evolved and closer to God whereas in the lower realms, the beings were more attached to material possessions.

For Sarvan's rational mind, this kind of description was nothing less than a fairytale. So, he did exactly what a rational person does when encountered with a situation like this.

'Shiv!' Sarvan called out, 'quickly come here, there is something that I want to show to you.'

Shiv jumped out from the back of the truck and came to Sarvan. When Shiv looked at the chart, he just kept looking at it for some time and then his facial expressions changed.

He took the chart from Sarvan's hand and kept on gazing at it. It was my time to get inside Shiv's brain to comprehend what exactly he was feeling.

When I peeped out of Shiv's eyes, he was not exactly looking at the image of the ordinary universe that had bewildered Sarvan. In fact, his gaze was stuck at a small image just adjacent to the main image.

The image also had Lord Vishnu lying down but in this image, there were thousands of bubbles that were coming out of a sleeping Vishnu as if they were air bubbles that Vishnu was breathing in and out.

And then suddenly, Shiv fell asleep.

Amidst the deep darkness on Shiv's slumber and the vividness of his abstract dreams the words uttered by Chit were echoing distinctly in his mind,' the universe is the same inside and outside. To find God, find the Map of the Universe.'

CHAPTER 13

THE MYSTERY OF GOD PICTURES

The shower of bullets and rudraksh arrows came from all sides and it came too soon, but they missed the family members as Sarvan had taken all of them inside the temple.

Shiv woke up seconds before Marich's gang was about to break open the temple door. He tied the Shree - Yantra on his forehead and stood in front of the door, covering the entire family.

At this moment, I was about to witness the grandest event since my inception. An event in which I was about to witness the evolution of a human into a superhuman. An event that will change my very perception about the creator and his creation. An event which was going to bring me closer to God.

To understand what Shiv understood, we need to understand the picture of Lord Pradhyuman.

When Shiv looked at the Golak Chart, his mind was fixated at the picture of Lord Vishnu, breathing in and out millions of air bubbles because Shiv was able to grasp the concept of Maha - Vishnu or the celestial man.

This can be understood by deciphering the deeply hidden secrets contained in the pictorial representation of Gods.

When Lord Vishnu is shown sleeping, it is a clear indication that he is in a dream state and the universe, as we know it, is just a figment of his imagination.

The navel of Lord Vishnu can be understood as the singularity from where everything in the universe has been born. If we correlate it with modern science, we can call it the starting point of the Big Bang. Singularity can be understood as the point of origin where everything had been concentrated before the universe was born; and suddenly, during the Big Bang, the universe exploded into existence. It has been represented like the lotus of creation that explodes out of the navel of Vishnu.

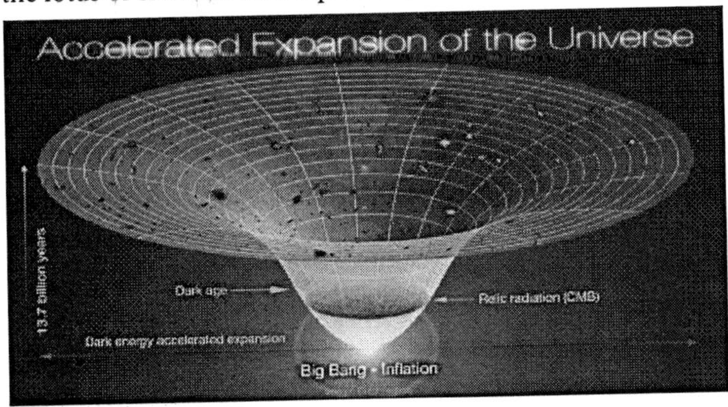

Lord Brahma sitting on the lotus represents the creation or everything in the universe.

When Lord Vishnu is sleeping, the lotus comes out of his navel and when he wakes up, the lotus along with Lord Brahma goes inside his navel again. This represents the infinite cycles of expansion and contraction which a universe undergoes. Even as per modern science the Big Bang will be succeeded by a Big Crunch. So, the lotus blooming out of Lord Vishnu's navel in his sleeping state represents that the universe gets created as a dream of Lord Vishnu and dissolves back into Lord Vishnu's navel when he wakes up from his sleep.

The serpent or the Nag with infinite hoods is the Shesha - Nag, on whose coil Lord Vishnu is resting. It is also called Adi - Ananta - Shesha - Nag. Adi means starting. Ananta means till the end. And Shesha means balance. If we think about the literal meaning, then it means' from starting till the end, whatever is in balance or left in between' ; in short, it means 'time'.

The hooded serpent, covering the sleeping Lord Vishnu, is symbolising that time is protective of the life of the universe. No one can finish anyone's life before the time the person gets over. We may say that our time is limited on this Earth, but in fact, whatever duration of life God has given you acts as immunity from death. The infinite hoods represent infinite timelines of the sixth - dimension based on the decisions taken by a person.

Lord Vishnu is floating on the Garbodaka Ocean, also known as Karna Sagar. It is an ocean created by brain waves or thoughts of Lord Vishnu himself. Every single water droplet in that ocean represents a unique universe. Every time Lord Vishnu inhales, he dissolves billions of universes and every time he exhales, he gives birth to billions of universes. This explains the concept of multiverse or parallel universes.

Every single bubble contained a unique ordinary universe of its own, with the image of Lord Vishnu and the lotus coming out of his navel representing the Big Bang taking place in every single bubble.

There are billions of universes existing at the same time, and in every single one of them, there are 14 worlds each. And among them, in the middle - level world, human beings exist in the form of three - dimensional beings.

The Goddess Maya is a representation of Nature or all kinds of materialistic worldly attractions. The Goddess pressing the feet of Lord Vishnu symbolically represents that till the time the universe is in existence, nature or the material world will provide for all comforts and will look after the needs of every person in the world.

But then, there remains one more character in the picture that remains unexplained.

If the serpent is time, Goddess Maya is material attractions, Lord Brahma is the universe, and Garbodaka Ocean is the multiverse, then who is Lord Vishnu?

The answer can be understood by a small tale where Lord Krishna, who was an incarnation of Lord Vishnu, during his childhood on Earth, consumed mud. His mother, Yashoda, saw him eating mud and told him to open his mouth. When Lord Krishna opened his mouth, Yashoda was able to see the entire universe in the mouth of Lord Krishna.

This learning reverberated with the words Chit had said –' Universe is inside as it is outside'.

How can it be possible? How can it be that in the human form, there is a complete universe present inside as it is outside?

There is only one explanation that can make it possible. The truth that Shiv was able to decipher in his deeply meditative sleeping state. It is only possible if you are Vishnu. Then, you create your own universe around you with your thoughts, your time on Earth is what keeps you alive, and your material possessions are what comfort you.

String theory is the most scientifically advanced theory existing today that aims to elucidate every phenomenon by one single explanation.

It is said to be a bridge between physics and quantum physics. The theory is based on the assumption that at a sub - atomic scale, which is even more microscopic than quartz, there are small loops of strings that are constantly vibrating and the nature of every single thing or force in the universe is a product of the nature of the vibration in the string or the shape it finally takes.

The millions of varieties of things existing in the physical world are just a product of arrangement of atoms despite an atom being primarily hollow in itself. Similarly, if we go to an even more microscopic level, then we realise that the nature of these atoms and even the forces of nature are a product of these strings.

So, the properties of a universe are not decided by these heavenly bodies or huge planets that we see, they are decided at a very microscopic level. There can be a complete galaxy inside a single atom. There can be a complete universe inside every person.

What needs to be understood is that with our thoughts and brainwaves, we can influence the behaviour and vibrations of these strings. So, we can create a complete universe around us just by our thoughts.

Shiv had only mastered one art in his despicable lifetime–of controlling and channelizing his thoughts and brainwaves. Until now, Shiv had learnt to channelize the energy flow in and around his own body. But this new knowledge made me again question if I am limiting myself in the confines of an indoctrinated mind.

'Why am I limiting myself to just channelizing energy when I can be the creator?' Shiv said. 'If I can concentrate energy to create an energy shield, then maybe I can concentrate it further to create matter.'

'Look deep within you, Shiv,' I said. You will have to feel the vibration of every single atom of your body in the same way that you feel your heartbeat. Feel your infinite self. Feel yourself as a storehouse of energy. Feel yourself as a complete universe.'

You are nothing but a bundle of energy held together by Consciousness and indoctrinated to believe that you are limited by the rules of the physical world. The more you will overcome fear, the more you will understand about your true self, and the more you will liberate yourself from the shackles of worldly laws.

People wait their entire lives looking for miracles in the outer world without realising that they themselves are the creators of miracles in their lives. The energy around them is shaped by their own brain waves and manifests in the form of physical matter in their lives. If one can control his thoughts and feelings, then he will have the power to shape or alter the physical reality around him.

Shiv's pineal gland was releasing hormones like an erupting volcano, as he was fighting a battle deep within his own mind.

'Aham Brahamasmi,' Shiv said. (I am Brahma, the creator). He was in deep contemplation with his eyes closed.

The doors broke opened and the militia of Marich's army poured inside the temple with their guns, spraying fuming lead in all directions.

The bullets hit against the energy shield created by Shiv and vanished into thin air. A hail of rudraksh arrows then pierced through the energy shield and accelerated towards Shiv. Shiv raised his fisted right hand and the arrows stopped in mid - air as if hovering by some invisible force. Shiv opened his fist and the arrows followed gravity to hit the ground.

Now, Shiv opened his eyes and the very next moment, he charged at the armed gunmen with lightning speed. A bare hand moving with high velocity has enough momentum to knock out a person in one blow. It hardly took a minute for Shiv to knock out the entire militia inside the temple to fall on the ground.

With the frontline pawns cleared, Shiv stepped out of the temple premise to face the kingpins.

Shiv raised both his hands in the air and filled his lungs to their maximum capacity and then, with full force, blew out air towards the assailants. The air he blew turned into a hurricane tossing off the aggressors like a pack of cards. The winds swirled into a tornado with a gust so severe that it even moved the monster truck parked to a side, but Aghora created an invisible bubble around himself and Marich, that prevented them from being blown away.

Aghora waved his stick in a circular motion to bring out three black shadows that leapts towards Shiv. The shadows looked like ghastly spirits famished for human blood. Shiv opened his palms and a globe of light appeared in his hands. The enormous light produced by the globe blinded the surrounding with its intensity. It was almost as if a sun of cold white light had descended into Shiv's hand. In no time, the black shadows disappeared as darkness disappears at the advent of light.

Now, Aghora and Marich split in different directions to divide Shiv's attention.

Aghora flung an array of small fireballs towards Shiv while running in a tangential direction. The fireballs grew in size as they accelerated towards Shiv. Shiv extended both his hands in front of his chest to create an energy shield.

The energy shield took on the energy of the massive fireball but the momentum of the impact threw Shiv on the ground.

One after another, an increasing number of fireballs started hitting the energy shield that had been created by Shiv and with every impact, the momentum of the impact kept increasing. It was becoming difficult for Shiv to hold on.

Marich, on the other side, took out something akin to a harpoon used to catch big fish and fired it towards Shiv. This time the harpoon pierced through the energy shield of the distracted Shiv and pierced through Shiv's left shoulder blade.

A moment of distraction on Shiv's part had allowed Marich to invade his protective wall.

Shiv cried out in pain as he sat with one knee on the ground, but continued to defend himself against the fireballs.

I was watching the inevitable defeat of truth with destitute scorn and repulsive bewilderment. It was déjà vu. The future was going to repeat itself.

While I was busy watching the scene outside, a strange new build - up was taking place inside Shiv's brain. I noticed it after some delay and was immediately taken aback by it.

Due to some unknown reason, there was new - fangled white light illuminating the ambience inside Shiv's brain. By the time I noticed it, the radiance had taken the shape of a white glow that looked identical in form and shape to me.

The white glow moved closer to me, and closer, till it started to mingle with me in a manner that made it become a part of me. The brilliant white photons of the surreal radiation started to circle around the tiny bluish photons that made my existence conceivable.

It looked as if I and the white glow were intermixing with each other and every single particle of my mystical body was dancing with the particles of the white glow.

I started to feel an electrifying energy pulsating through every part of my existence. I began to feel myself to be a corpse who had just been brought back to life. I felt a surge of newly found Consciousness, an out - worldly experience as if I was being elevated to a realm of extraordinary power and empowering bliss. I felt as if I had just been completed.

Shiv got up as if he no longer felt the pain of the harpoon splitting his shoulder blade. His face had an expression of tranquillity but deep inside his brain,the hormones released by his pineal gland had empowered my fusion - form with the white light.

Shiv raised his hands and with Aghora and Marich looking in dismay, multiple arms came out of Shiv's side. Shiv grew in size until he towered over the temple in the background. He took out the harpoon from his shoulder and broke it like a matchstick. In every hand of Shiv, different weapons started emerging. Shiv was looking terrifying at this moment.

Shiv lifted two of his arms and hammered the ground with his fist. Marich and Aghora fell down by the trembles created on the ground by the impact.

Aghora got up and took out a powdered substance from his bag. Aghora threw the substance on the ground and all of a sudden, a storm of sand rose from the ground that completely obscured Shiv's view.

When the storm subsided, Aghora and Marich along with their army of goons had vanished.

As Shiv subdued, his size reduced to normal and the extra arms disappeared. Shiv was exhausted as his human body was not used to being under the command of such enormous metaphysical powers that he had just experienced.

I was perplexed. The white glow now disentangled from me into a separate identity that stood before me, now with a serenity that was distinctly different from the energised form that I have experienced.

'Who are you, divine power?' I asked with utmost gratitude.

The white gaseous form moved a little bit as if trying to get into shape and then I heard the heavenly female voice, 'I am Shakti. Without Shakti, Shiv (Lord Shiva) is nothing but a Shav (corpse).'

I was astounded and spell bound by the answer. I was witnessing the real divinity, the Goddess herself in person.' May I ask you, Goddess, how did you come to know that I needed your help?'

'I knew because I was accompanying you all along. I am the Consciousness that guides Vani,' Shakti said.

CHAPTER 14

THE CONSCIOUSNESS RNANUBANDHANAN

I was astonished like a blinded rabbit in front of the mystical white power that had helped me win the fight against Marich and Aghora. Of course, it was all happening in a metaphysical realm inside the head of Shiv.

'You what?' I snapped.

'I am the Consciousness that guides Vani,' the white mystical power repeated.

'But why would you help me? You should be inside Vani's head like I stay inside Shiv's head. How did you manage to get inside Shiv's head and mingle with me?' I asked.

'I did that the same way you jump from one head to another.' she was aware that I was simultaneously connected to many heads.' What I have understood is that a Consciousness can jump between brains whose destinies are connected,' she concluded.

'But how is Shiv in any way connected with the destiny of Vani? And even if they are connected, why am I not able to get inside the mind of Vani?' I asked.

My gaseous Goddess trembled as if laughing on me, 'Well, of course, Vani's destiny is connected to Shiv's destiny. I am the connection. I am the Consciousness that was guiding Shiv's mother when the cruel hands of fate took her away.'

In a day full of life - changing surprises, this one completely knocked me off.

'You were Shiv's mother!' I cried, 'How is that possible? How did you know that Vani would one day meet Shiv?'

'It's a long story. There was a Superconsciousness that guided me,' the Goddess said. 'I gave Vani the intuition to visit Rohan's place when Shiv was there. I also ensured that Vani leaves the Shree - Yantra on Shiv's forehead and balanced the energies in Shiv's Ajna Chakra.'

I was suddenly reminded of Chit, the Super - consciousness that was helping me all along.

There are Superconsciousnesses between God and humans that help in framing human life as per the design of God and enacting destinies into effect. They are the Consciousnesses that guide demigods, saints, gurus etc.

These Consciousnesses do not have absolute knowledge, but being multi - dimensional beings, they are much more aware than an average human mind or any lower Consciousness. They serve the sole purpose of establishing Dharma or guiding people to the righteous path or the path chosen by God.

Every human being has the capability to rise to the level of these demigods or saints by adequately enhancing his knowledge and perception about the self and the supreme.

That is the reason we sometimes find enlightened beings in this world.

There are too many imposters. But if one can find a truly enlightened being as his guru, then he can experience the joys of the world oblivious to mankind.

'I knew that one day Vani would be the one who will cross the destiny of Shiv,' the Goddess continued. 'After my death as Shiv's mother, I was concerned about Shiv as he was just a baby. In that time of grief, I found a supreme being in the form of a Superconsciousness who guided me to Vani. When the love between Rohan and Vani was brewing, I got to understand you. Since you are the same Consciousness that resides in both Rohan and Shiv, it became possible for me to mingle with you at the time of dire need.'

'How did you die?' I asked. 'I heard Marich saying that he had murdered Shiv's mother.'

'How do you know that and when did you speak to Marich?' she was surprised.

Of course, how would she know about the innumerable time loops that I had undergone while trying to amend the pastin the fight against evil to ensure a better present in some other parallel universe?

Except me, no one else was privy to the happenings inside the hellish lab of Marich, where he had taken all the family members captive. I was the only one who had knowledge of the future that would have resulted had the events gone even minutely different.

'Well, like you, even I have a few secrets. Let's just say I know that Marich is Shiv's father and also the murderer of Shiv's mother. The question is why did he kill Shiv's mother?' I was inquisitively perturbed.

'Shiv's mother was a nurse in a hospital in the city of Mumbai in India,' the Goddess started the story. 'It all started when one night, after completing her duty hours, she was trying to catch a bus to her home. While she was waiting at the bus stand there was an accident on the road where a car was crushed by a raging truck and all three boys in that truck died.'

'Wait, this entire scene you have described sounds familiar to me,' I said, cutting her story. 'My first encounter in this human world was inside a boy named Raghu and I was the witness to this exact scenario that you are describing. Raghu died in that accident. I died in that accident.'

The Goddess was a little taken aback by the revelation. 'So that's how they are connected. Sometimes it marvels me how the creator has connected different life stories of these mortal humans together. So many people from so different parts of the world can suddenly find their lives intermingled due to some strangely woven web of destiny,' she said.

'See, I need to know what happened to Shiv's mother? I believe that the clue to defeating Marich lies within the mystery of Shiv's mother's death,' I said.

'Her name was Naina, she was the most compassionate human being I have ever known and hence, her profession of a nurse did full justice to her nobility. But the night Naina took the causalities of that accident to the hospital, her life changed forever.

While she was sitting inside the ambulance, there was one patient who remained in a semi - conscious state for some time. That person confided Naina with certain secrets that he wanted someone to know before he died,' the Goddess said.

'I remember that now. It was indeed Raghu. I remember him blabbering certain things to the nurse in the ambulance,' I said.

'I couldn't exactly comprehend what he was saying but he was talking about the ill effects of certain drugs and that those evil drugs had driven him and his friends towards crime,' Goddess said.

I suddenly remembered the slight yellowish injection that Raghu and his friends used to inject. Was it possible that under the influence of those drugs, their pineal gland was destroyed and then their brains were controlled by means of other chemicals? Marich had mentioned about the existence of such drugs, but could they have been used to drive aggressive and criminal tendencies in human beings?

'The Goddess continued with her story.' the patient died after sometime but Naina decided to investigate the matter in detail. She examined all the three dead bodies and found traces of a strange substance in their brain that was making the brain emit unusual patterns in the report.

Naina examined the substances and was able to decipher the exact compound. It was a narcotic drug locally manufactured by illegally mixing a few common medical drugs to produce an evil compound. The real problem started later when she detected the presence of the same evil compound in many of the common drugs that were being prescribed by the doctors in that hospital.

Interestingly, she later detected that the drugs containing that evil compound belonged to a single medicine production company with the name 'TRIPURA PHARMACEUTICALS PVT LTD'.

No prize for guessing that the CEO of Tripura Pharmaceuticals was none other than Mr. Marich Natraj.

By the time Marich learnt about Naina's misadventure, she had already written a letter to the Medical Council of India with the details of the case and asked for a probe into the matter.

Marich was able to control the damage at higher levels but at the lower level, Naina took the matter to press to get the medical company blacklisted. This rattled Marich as the reputation of his company was on stake, but despite diplomatic outreach, Naina was not ready to budge.' the Goddess paused for a while.

'Maybe Shiv has taken some values of his mother,' I commented.

The Goddess continued, 'There was only one way to stop Naina. Marich kidnapped Naina and kept her in a basement at his residence. But he did not just kill her. Marich had something more in mind. In the small basement with no window, Marich kept Naina enslaved for over a year.

To make Naina submit to his dominance, Marich raped Naina several times; most of the time, after subduing her with drugs. She was offered very little food and a little water per day. But despite the inhuman torment, Marich was not able to break Naina's will to live. She was a fighter and she fought on.

It is true that Marich is Shiv's father, but Shiv is an illegitimate child. He was a product of the violent assaults by which Marich raped his mother.

But once Shiv was conceived, Naina loved Shiv very much. She was always worried about the effect this forced injection of drugs might have on her child. Marich had presumed that Shiv would die in the womb but to his surprise, Shiv took birth.

Even his aide, Aghora, was surprised to find the resoluteness of the child when several of his tantra - mantra had less impact on Shiv than they would have on even a normal human being.

They decided to take Shiv as a subject for their drug tests, but Naina got a hint of their intentions.

One day, Naina planned her escape. She broke a splint from her metallic bed and sharpened it into a weapon.

When Marich came inside, she slit his face and ran away with her child. The scar you see today on Marich's face was made by Naina, no one else could ever come that close to Marich.

Unfortunately, Aghora was able to track her just as she was moving out of the house. She fought with Aghora with the splint in one hand and a baby in another, but soon, more bodyguards arrived.

Naina was caught and brought back drenched with blood from the wounds Aghora and his men had inflicted on her in front of Marich. Marich slit her throat while she was still holding her baby.

Even after dying, she left a debt on me–her Consciousness. The debt to look after her baby, and for Naina's sake, I kept doing it. I had to find a way to strengthen Shiv and I found it when you found a way to swap between Rohan and Shiv's brains. ondered for a while and said the Goddess paused after that.

'I pondered for a while and said,' so that is why,on our first interaction itself, Shiv told me that I am connected to other bodies.'

'I could visit Shiv only during his deep meditative state, that's why when he was looking to teleport you, I guided him to Rohan's mind,' she said.

By the time our conversation ended, Shiv had fainted due to physical and mental exhaustion.

PART II – NATURE (PRAKRITI)

CHAPTER 15

THE GOD's DILEMMA

While Shiv was in an unconscious state, I meditated for Chit at arrive, and after remembering him for just a few hours, I found him by my side. As bad as the situation maybe, his sight was an assurance to me that everything will be all right.

'Why is there so much evil in the human world, Chit? And why does evil become so powerful?' I spoke as soon as I saw Chit.

'Duality is a dilemma of the creator and an imperative of creation,' Chit began to explain. 'When the creator wanted to create the universe, he faced a dilemma.

The dilemma is that creation is relative. For creation to take place, first there had to be something uncreated.

If God wants to create something long, he will have to create something short in comparison. Long cannot be defined without having something short in comparison.

For God to create a positive there has to be a negative, otherwise positive cannot exist. If the entire universe has only positive charge, then positive is uncreated. To justify the existence of positive, God has to create a negative in comparison.

Hot can only be felt if one has experienced comparative coldness at some point intime. If the world has only one temperature, then hot has just not been created. No one would understand that hot exists.

How can you call a person tall or short without having a comparative opposite? So, for every light there will be a dark, for everything warm there will be something cold and for every good there will be bad.' Chit stopped.

'But then what empowers the bad? They seem to be getting stronger than the good,' I asked.

Chit grew in size as he does when he is about to reveal a secret and said,' there are two ways of getting superhuman powers: the first is the Sattvik way and the other is the Tamsik Way.

The Sattvik way of getting powers is through yogic practices like the recitation of mantras, meditation, devotion etc. This is the path defined by the rules of Dharma. This is the way that has been recommended by various Avatars of God.

However, there is another way of achieving these powers by a shorter but extremely dangerous way.

That is by way of Tantrik practices. However, there are severe repercussions of adopting this way as the negative karmas strike back at you.

'Whether it is through Mantra or Tantra, the powers can be drawn from only one source that is Lord Shiva,' Chit said.

'What do you mean by Avtars?' I asked. It was a name I had heard for the first time.

'Avatars are incarnations of God. See, whenever a soul enters this world called Maya, it has to take a body. So, by this logic, there should be no difference between God and humans as they are both souls surrounded by a body,' Chit said.

'Correct, so how will a God be born? Last time you told me something about God being a set of waves, I got really puzzled.'

'The difference lies in the possession of Consciousness,' Chit said.' Once the vessel of a human body is prepared, it gets activated by the power of the soul. But there is another super cosmic entity that combines with the above two to get life into existence. That is Consciousness.

A soul's life journey in Maya is guided throughout by Consciousness. However, the soul has the choice to listen or ignore that advice. That is why it is the soul that gets punished or rewarded for its actions or karmas in this world. But you and me, we are always there.

The difference between God and a human is that God is guided by God's Consciousness. They get all their powers as they are more aware about their true infinite nature.

These powers that I talk about are nothing but knowledge. The moment you come to know that a human body need not abide by the physical and assumed laws of nature, you become powerful, Chit said.

'But Chit, how do you know all of this? Have you seen God?' I asked.

The gaseous form of Chit appeared as if smiling at the innocence of my question.' Oh yes, in times of great misery upon this world, God himself came down to guide those who were righteous. I have myself served him and will continue to do so whenever he comes back. He was called Shree - Ram.' Chit's answer shook the innermost cell or atom or wave or whatever I had in me.

'Who are you, Chit? And why are you helping me?' I asked in amazement.

'Well, I am helping you because that is what I do. I help those who believe in me. I come to the call of those who call me with their true heart. I am known by many names, but in the human world, I am more famous by the name Hanuman,' Chit said.

If I had a mouth, I would have screamed. If I had legs, I would have fallen on my knees. If I had a heart, it would have stopped beating. If I had life, I would have fainted. All this while, it was Lord Hanuman himself guiding me.

'You are Hanuman?' I asked after recovering.

'No, I am the Consciousness that guided Hanuman. He was a Godly soul who had Godly powers. He has left his body but his soul will prevail till the end of this world,' Chit or Lord Hanuman told me.

'If you have been associated with God, why did you allow evil to rule the world?' I asked.

'Human beings have this illusion that with evil or aggression, they can rule. However, that is not how Prakriti works. Prakriti works according to its own laws,' Chit said.

'And what is the Law of Nature?' I asked.

'Let me help you understand nature and its laws,' Chit said. 'Imagine a vast ocean of spirits. Out of them, only a handful will take birth. Out of this handful, only a tiny droplet measure of spirits will be getting the gift of Consciousness and will take birth in a human form. Rest will live as plants, animals, reptiles etc. The balance will forever live in the spirit form without ever experiencing the most divine creation of God, Nature.

Nature is God in its very real existence. It is the fulfiller of all your prayers, it is the answer toall your problems. It is the beginning of the enigma of life and it is the conclusion of every quest. Nature is the reason the cycle of birth and the law of karma exist. Nature is the reason that you want to possess and indulge, that you want to be born again or live forever. It's the keeper of the deepest secrets. It's the provider of great treasures. There is nothing more divine than what we can experience with our senses, nothing more pacifying or more mystifying than the natural surroundings. It is the protector and the punisher. It is the mother and the child.

On the surface, nature appears to be a non - responsive entity. It appears to be vulnerable to human interference. And this attribute has resulted in the conquest of mankind to control nature.

In human society, this control over nature manifests itself in the form of power. The more nature you can control, the more powerful you are. This perceived power creates an imaginary world around us which is called Maya, wherein we feel that we can control the nature around us while the reality is that we can't.

The real secret is much deeper. Nature is not just a hypothetical entity; it has a soul. It sets rules for everything that takes birth in it. You live with a myth that it is you who is ensuring your survival, but in fact, nature ensures that you don't have to worry about survival,' Chit said and continued. 'Just imagine, have you ever wondered why seemingly invincible creatures of the wild have always figured on top of the list of endangered species while the most humble and vulnerable species have always survived against all odds.

Nature is full of various species which thrive on each other for their survival and form a food chain in which every link eats the one below it and is eaten by the link above it.

What is interesting, however, is that the species at the bottom of this food chain, who are considered most vulnerable, are the ones with the best survivability rate. If we look closely we will find that the species at the top of this food chain are the ones which we generally find on the endangered list.

There was a time when Earth was ruled by the ferocity of the mammoth Dinosaurs. So imposing was their existence that thousands of years later, their absolute domination over every other existing species of that time still provides motivation for filmmakers to imagine and recreate that era on the celluloid. Yet, their existence today can only be ascertained by the skeletal remains preserved in a few museums around the world.

The aquatic life has been ruled for centuries by predators like sharks and crocodiles with almost no threat whatsoever from any other creature. Yet, today most of the shark and crocodile species figure in the list of endangered species around the world.

A tiger has no natural enemy in the wild. He reigns supreme and is aptly called'the King of the Jungle'. And yet, there is a worldwide campaign to save tigers.

Compare that to approximately 50 billion chicken and more than 99 billion tons of fish killed every year for human consumption alone. Yet, the numbers of fish and chicken can be regulated by simple processes. The almost unregulated killing of chicken and fish has not yet forced them into extinction. They can be bred anywhere. They are easy to multiply.

Don't you feel that nature empowers the weak? Don't you think nature provides the weak with a protective mechanism that will see them prevail despite being temporarily vulnerable against the attacker?

Why does it happen that all attempts by human beings to win against mosquitoes have in fact made today's mosquitoes stronger than ever?

Why is it that the process of evolution seems so easy and simple with these lowly creatures rather than the formidable ones?

A lion or a whale will find it difficult to survive anywhere other than their natural habitat whereas a cow or a goat can be taken almost anywhere in the world with considerable ease.

When the Earth went over an Apocalypse, the tiny cockroach braved it out against forces of destruction and still lives on as one of the oldest species of this planet.

In fact, what we perceive as a weakness is in fact strength from nature's point of view. To understand it, let's once again take the common example of a tiger and a goat.

Tiger is more powerful. It runs faster. It can eat a goat for its survival whereas a goat feeds on grass, looks fragile, moves slower, has no fangs and hence, appears weak. A normal conclusion would be that the tiger is a stronger species than the goat. However, as per the Law of Nature, it is the reverse.

Tiger needs goat for its existence; the goat doesn't need tiger. While grass is in abundance and easy to get, a tiger has to work hard to get a goat. They are difficult and rare to catch and as the tiger keeps feeding on the weakest goats, overtime, it becomes harder and harder for the tiger to catch a goat.

The second aspect is copulation. The goat can reproduce easily while the tiger has a low fertility rate. And worse, at the time of birth, the tigress can get so overpowered by hunger that she can eat her cubs. Her ferocity goes out of her control.

Hence, from nature's point of view, while the tiger may appear to be stronger than a goat, it will eventually be engulfed by its own ferocity.' Chit ended his monologue leaving me bewildered.

'But if this is how nature defines strength, then is it applicable to the human world also? And how?' I was now opening up to Chit.

'Nature deals with the human world in exactly the same

manner. The history of human civilisation is the history of some magnificent empires that have time and again established an unchallenged dominance around the world.

There was a time when the Roman Empire was so imposing in its existence that even the maps of those time depict Roman Empire covering almost the entire Earth with a few patches of land left for the balance of the world. The magnificence of the Egyptian empire can be ascertained by the audacity of its huge structures and architectural wonders.

The Persians, the Greeks, the Portuguese are some of the multifarious empires that reigned the world with a remarkable presence and yet, today they exist only in wrecked ruins scattered in patches standing as mute testimony to the people who thought they could rule over the laws of nature. Then came the kingdoms of France, Britain, and now in the last around 70 years, it's USA.

On the other hand, there are countries like India and China. These countries have been non - aggressive throughout their historical accounts. They have been subjected to years of foreign dominance and a deliberate policy of changing the cultural backbone of these primarily religious countries. Yet today, these countries are the cradle to a third of humanity and are rising fast to establish their place in the world. These civilisations are somewhere still connected to their ancient wisdom and slowly these countries are again finding their cultural heritage.

Almost 1000 years of world dominance and unchallenged economic exploitation by European nations and after just 70 years since that colonisation ended, the European countries again find themselves in a whirlpool of saturated economies, unemployed youth, decaying growth rate, and a population that is turning atheist.

Hence, a natural conclusion can be drawn that what we perceive as a weaker species is empowered by nature to survive longer.

The economically and socially deprived women are simply

more empowered by nature to reproduce more than the economically better ones.

Children who play in mud grow up to be stronger than those who play on an indoor carpet. Those who drink distilled water are more prone to diseases than those drinking river water. That's the nature's way,' Chit said.

'You mean to say that even though evil may look invincible, in the end, nature will make the good one win. But who will decide what is good and what is evil?' I asked.

Chit wobbled as if laughing on me and said, 'You decide that.'

CHAPTER 16

THE FOURTEEN WORLDS

From his trans - meditative state, Shiv suddenly woke up as if awoken by a bad dream.' Where is Vani?'

All members looked around each other with an astounded gaze.

'Last I saw, she was inside the temple,' Rohan's mother said.

Shiv and Rohan ran to the temple.

Vani was lying unconscious at the foot of the giant idol of Lord Padmanabha inside the temple.

Rohan lifted up Vani and made her lie on her back till she gained Consciousness.

All the family members were acting strange while sitting in a circle inside the temple. Santy was lying unconscious ever since he saw Shiv growing multiple arms. Rohan's mother was sitting on the other side of the idol with her eyes closed and mumbling some prayers in her aloofness. The events they had witnessed in the last 24 hrs had changed something inside them. It had changed their very perspective on life.

They had not yet fully comprehended as to what had happened and what they had seen but they were aware that there are certain bigger powers at play here. They could feel the difference of their expanded Consciousness inside their minds but they could not describe it. They could hear the voice and the words that their subconscious mind was trying to tell them but they could not fully understand them.

Because in the last 24 hrs, everyone's Consciousness had lived in a metaphysical realm and experienced out of the world realities that their physical bodies could not comprehend. So they were quite not ready to fully absorb what they had just been through.

Shiv was the first to speak. He got up and moved in front of Vani, who was sitting on an elevated platform with Rohan to her side.

As Vani looked on, Shiv sat on one knee in front of her, removed the Shree - Yantra from his head and said, 'You may find it strange or you may not even believe me, but you are the reason because of whom I was able to defeat Marich in this fight.

It is difficult for me to explain to you how I am connected to you, but just know that in this finite world, you are the Goddess that I will forever worship. Till the time I am alive I will protect and defend your honour with every last breath of mine.' With that, Shiv placed the Shree - Yantra at Vani's feet. 'Allow me to present a symbol of my powers as a tribute to your worthy existence.'

Shiv kept the Shree - Yantra band and then bowed down and touched his forehead to her feet as a mark of respect. Then Shiv again knelt, joined both his hands, and said' Namah - asi - te (namaste = I bow to the God within you).' With that, Shiv left the temple.

Tears rolled down Vani's eyes due to some uncontrolled emotions that was bubbling inside her ever since she had seen this guy for the first time. But after what Shiv said, she was not able to control anymore and cried for reasons she could not fathom.

Sarvan, who was the quietest till now, moved close to Vani. Then he held her face gently between both his palms and looked deep into her eyes. Tears were hysterically rolling down her eyes.

'I love you!' Sarvan said to Vani. 'I have realised that I love you enough to value your happiness above my selfish needs. I am sorry for all the time of your life you wasted trying to stitch the tatters of my life into a household. But now, I know how to set things right. Would you believe me this one last time?'

Vani nodded a yes.

'I want you to start a new life; a new life with Rohan. I want you to live, love, and dream once again,' Sarvan said.

Vani shrugged in disbelief.' You don't know what you are saying, Sarvan. You are not in your senses. Marriage is forever,' Vani said, sobbing uncontrollably now.

'I was tuned to live my life as per the rules and procedures of the society even when they drove me to madness,' Sarvan said, 'but in the last one day of my life, I have broken every rule of this and even other worlds.

I have experienced powers that I never knew existed and I have travelled to dimensions inaccessible to human existence.

After all that I have experienced, it is not possible for me to be tied down by the rules of this finite world. I want to discover the infinite. I want to experience the limits of my Consciousness. I want to be more than anyone in this world has ever been.

I want to go beyond the permissible limits of any relationship, particularly marriage. That was the reality that I wanted to understand when we separated, and finally, I feel as if I am on the correct path. You are and will be the only women I love, but my love for you will not be physical. It will be beyond the rules of physics. But I want you to live a normal life that you deserve to live with Rohan. I have noticed the chemistry between you two ever since I first met him. I have seen his love for you in his eyes. I have seen him protecting you even with his life. As a friend or a lover, there is no one who can understand or love you better than Rohan.'

'Rohan, will you take care of this beautiful lady all your life?' Sarvan asked while kissing Vani on her forehead.

Rohan had forever waited to say this to Vani and today he did that under the most unusual circumstances, 'I ….. I …' Rohan was stammering.

'He will!' Everyone turned in the direction of Rohan's mother.

'Rohan was never the same ever since you left; there is no one else who can fill the void in my son's life like you,' Rohan's mother said and placed Vani's hand into Rohan's hand.

'I am giving you my love, Rohan, take care of her,' Sarvan said with a smile. Vani was silently sobbing at the emotional turmoil the turn of events were causing inside her.

In the living room of a lavish farm house situated on an isolated hill in a remote location amidst a thick jungle, Marich and Aghora sat on a plush sofa facing each other with grim looks on their faces.

'I fail to understand how is that possible?' Aghora said. 'I had calculated everything. He seems to be possessing amazing powers that he can summon in almost no time. It has been just three days since he has risen from an autistic body and today, he is mastering Siddh is like a veteran. How can he master this ancient knowledge in such a short span of time?'

'I have a different question in my mind.' Marich finally broke his silence 'How did he move the entire family inside the temple before we arrived? It seemed as if they were able to predict our move. But how?'

Aghora pondered over the question for some time. 'It seems he is playing us by creating some kind of an illusion. Otherwise, how was he aware of the rudraksh arrows? There is also something about the other family members that I am not able to understand, especially that software engineer and his wife; they seem to know something. I will have to find out.'

Aghora took Marich to another room where a Yagna was arranged and the fire was burning. They sat around the fire and chanted some mantras for some time. Aghora took out powder from a small pouch attached to his waist and with the utterance of some mantras, he threw it inside the fire. There was a loud hissing noise and a cloud of black smoke started coming out of the fire. The cloud soon took an almost human shape with ghastly eyes made of fire.

'I have summoned you here to find the truth behind the happenings in our recent past. Go and find out the reason behind Shiv's powers,' Aghora commanded the spirit.

The spirit made a hissing sound and flew out of the window, mixing into the dark of the night.

'I will ensure that the next time we meet with Mr. Shiv, he will not be able to spring any more surprises on us,' Aghora declared. 'Be prepared for an astonishing climax to this spectacular tale, be prepared for the most magnificent showdown.'

In the clear moonlit night, Shiv was sitting silently under the banyan tree deeply lost in his thoughts when Santy came and sat next to him. It was the first time in this timeline that Santy had overcome his inhibitions to close - up to Shiv.

'How did you do it?' Santy asked.

'Do what?' Shiv asked.

'Don't act ignorant,' Santy complained. 'You have to tell me how you expanded your size, grew many arms, made that transparent dome and performed all those miracles. By God dude, I was hell scared; but now when I think about it, you seem like a superhero straight from comic books.'

'I did the same to them what the world does with other humans,' Shiv said. 'I created an illusion of matter in a manner that scared them.'

'What! You mean that you never actually grew arms and size, it just looked to them that you did?' Santy said.

'When you polish a shoe, you just make its surface smoother so that light gets reflected better off from its surface. It doesn't change the shoe much; it just changes what has reached your eye.

Tall, big, and strong are just perceptions of the brain created by the inferences drawn from the inputs given by the Indriyans. What one can see or hear is what he will believe as reality. If I can distort the vision of a human being just a little bit so that he sees everything bigger, he will live believing that he is the smallest being on Earth. In reality, it was not that he was short, it was only that his vision was faulty. So, our perception of reality is created by whatever our Indriyans feed us,' Shiv said.

'So, in reality, did you grow arms and grow taller in size or not?' Santy again asked.

Shiv smiled a little and spoke with a calm demeanour.' We humans have become so limited by our own imagination that we have stopped understanding our own true self.

The society we live in has programmed us so much that we have reduced ourselves to become mere machines. We have locked our original powers and imagination in a prison; or should I say; we are the prison.

My solitary confinement during my childhood had completely cut me off from the influence of society. But now I feel that it happened for my good. In a way, it helped as I never got programmed. I remained my original self, maybe that is why this understanding comes easily to me. What I did were no miracles, it was just that my understanding about myself is maybe slightly better than yours.'

'What kind of understanding?' Santy asked, with an innocent face.

'Let me tell you something interesting. You know there was an amazing discovery I made just before the goons entered the temple. That this universe outside and inside the human body is the same,' Shiv said.

Santy got confused.' What do you mean? I have a Sun and stars inside me?'

'More than that, Santy, much...much more than that.' Shiv moved closer to Santy and looked directly into his eyes with an excited smile and said,' Not just stars; you have fourteen worlds inside you.'

'Whoah...fourteen worlds...how?' Santy exclaimed.

'The universe described by Goloka Chart had fourteen worlds

with the human world right in the centre, seven worlds below the human world, and six worlds above it. Now, let us try to relate the metaphor with the human body.

The human body has seven chakras. Consider that every single chakra corresponds with one world. Then that particular chakra is also the level where all the powers of that world can be unfolded. So now, the relative levels can be considered as follows: -

- Satyaloka corresponds to Sahasrara Chakra
- Tapaloka corresponds to Ajna Chakra
- Janaloka corresponds to Vishuddhi Chakra
- Maharloka corresponds to Anahata Chakra
- Svarloka corresponds to Manipura Chakra
- Bhuvarloka corresponds to Shvadhishthana Chakra
- Bhurloka corresponds to Muladhara Chakra

The ultimate aim of human life is spiritual rise. With spiritual rise, you reach higher worlds or higher chakras and the powers of those worlds or chakras keep getting unfolded within you.

But there is a strange omission. What about the lower seven worlds? Why are they less talked about and why aren't there any levels related to that in the human body? After all, these so - called lower worldshave been described to be full of opulence and richness. What will happen if we descend down into the lower worlds?

Human attachment to material possessions is the primary reason for descending down at these levels or to the lower worlds. This has been the defining characteristic of these worlds. Despite wealth and worldly possessions, the beings of these worlds live without the light of spiritual awakening and are, thus, forever caught in the web of suffering.

Perhaps, that is why these lower worlds have not been defined in the human body; because chakras only relate to spiritual enlightenment and not to material downfall.

So, if we have to spiritually ascent towards higher powers, then we will have to move away from material attachments. And what is the biggest material attachment of the human world?' Shiv paused for Santy to answer.

'Uh…biggest attachment…money or family…I don't know… you tell me?' Santy said.

'Even I am looking for the right answer, but I am sure that the day I find the answer to that, I will also find God,' Shiv said.

Two dark evil shadows were hidden amidst the darkness of the figure of the tree embossed by the silver moonlight. As Shiv and Santy spoke to each other, the shadows slowly crept forward and entered through Shiv's nostrils into Shiv's brain. It was like a virus gaining access to the main database computer, which contained the access to the knowledge stored inside Shiv's brain.

'She was the only female friend I was ever close to,' Rohan told Sarvan in a cautious and defensive tone,' maybe that's why I am a little protective about her; but I fully understand and honour the fact that she was your wife.'

Sarvan was reclining on a pillar inside the temple, facing the idol of Lord Pradhyuman and smiled at the words spoken by Rohan.

'You see, buddy, a few years back, maybe I would have killed you for even staring at my wife. But there is something that has happened in the last few days that has made me…how should I say... It has made me kind of fearless.'

'I am just not afraid of losing anything; neither my life nor any other being associated with me because I have experienced the world of energies. What we call emotions, be it love, jealousy, anger, and hate–they are just different vibrations mixing with the vibrations of our brain.' Sarvan looked into the eyes of Rohan and continued,' Do you remember that story from Lord Krishna's life where, in the town of Vrindavan, he used to simultaneously dance with hundreds of gopis (female devotees)? Do you understand the greater meaning that he conveyed?

Normally, it is impossible for any human being to be present at more than one place at the same time, however, Lord Krishna seemed to be creating an illusion of dancing with all the gopis concurrently. How can that be possible?'

Sarvan smiled as he spoke again, 'It is possible because even in his human form, Lord Krishna was aware that he is the manifestation of an infinite and omnipresent energy. If for a moment we stop considering Krishna as human and consider him to be a source of energy, the mystery of this dance becomes easy to understand.

Consider an energy form like the Sun. Sun as a form of energy can spread its sunlight and touch all the people at a place with the same warmth; Lord Krishna could be there with all the gopis at the same time and evoke the same emotion of love in all of them, without them feeling jealous of each other.

The catch in this story is that maybe the gopis of Vrindavan were the ones to witness the infinite form of Lord Krishna much before Arjun saw it in the battle of Mahabharata.

What people think of as leela or a 'dance of love', in reality was Lord Krishna imparting the lessons of immortality and eternal bliss to the gopis of Vrindavan.

Even today, it is said in Vrindavan that those gopi's are immortal and still dance with Lord Krishna in the same place at night. That is because of the Law of Conservation of Energy. Energy can neither be created nor be destroyed. So, if Krishna was an embodiment of a universal energy, then he is forever present. I want to experience that power Rohan. I want to feel that energy that the gopi's got addicted to and that liberated them.

Rohan, do you know that every colour has a vibration? We are affected by colour because it causes different effects on our psychology or emotions and even our health.

When we go down on a sub - atomic level, we do not find matter. It is only pure energy. According to quantum physics, everything is vibration. Everything is energy and energy is vibration. Therefore, everything in this world emits a certain vibrational frequency; even thoughts and feelings.

Emotions have unique vibrations just like colours and physical objects do. These emotional vibrations also go from higher (faster) to lower (slower). When you are laughing and having fun, your body's vibrations are faster. When you are tired and sick, your vibrations are slower. When you are in love, you feel energized. You feel like you are walking on a cloud. That is because your emotions are literally adding voltage and power to make your body feel light and energetic; and when you are negative and depressed, you feel sluggish, low and heavy.

We are the source that releases the vibrational energy that forms our existence. That is why we are our own creators.

Unknowingly, our thoughts and feelings create a magnetic field of fortune or misfortune around us. Whatever positive or negative energy we feel around us, their waves have been created in the past by us. It is very important to realize the fact that no one else is the decision maker of your destiny in this universe except yourself. There is no power that decides our destiny; we create our own destiny. We alone are responsible for the rose flowers or the thorns that we have in our lives. God gives you a wild forest. You have to convert it into a garden. He gives you only stones and other raw materials; you have to construct statues out of it.

'I want to experience this God like power.' Sarvan said.

Sarvan had a glitter in his eyes as if he had been possessed by the enlightenment of spiritual knowledge that he was receiving. He didn't seem to be bothered about his announcement of leaving his wife to another man. Rohan realised the futility of this conversation with Sarvan and resolved to look after Vani.

While Rohan and Sarvan were having this conversation, another pair of shadowy figures slowly crept forward and entered the bodies of Rohan and Sarvan through their nostrils without them realising it.

CHAPTER 17

THE MAP OF THE UNIVERSE

Aghora was sitting in the asana pose with his legs crossed, eyes closed, and a stone like stillness on his face in front of the yagna fire. Marich was brooding in deep thought on the opposite side of the fire when the window panes started fluttering. The fluttering grew intense as the window pane started banging as if trying to break away. The light in the room instinctively grew dim and four shadows entered the room hugging the floor and dissolved themselves into the Havana kund(the pit where yagna fire was burning).

Aghora suddenly opened his eyes completely wide and gazed deep into the fire muttering some mantras and threw a powdery substance into the fire. With a deep hissing noise, the flames of the yagna fire took the shape of three human figures standing side by side.

As Marich looked on, Aghora started interacting with the fiery figures in some strange language. In between the conversation, he used to throw a powdery substance into the fire. The fiery figures seemed to be fighting with each other and angrily muttering something that only Aghora could understand. The ritual went on for hours and then Aghora went completely quiet. The fiery figures disappeared into the fire and the fire doused off. The dim lights of the room came to their full luminescence.

'We may have underestimated their powers,' Aghora finally spoke to Marich,' there are factors which we did not consider while evaluating their clout.'

'What kind of factors? Do you want to tell me that Shiv has a hidden reserve of powers?' Marich asked.

'It is more than that. I have realised that we may just be targeting the wrong person. It is not just Shiv; all six of them are contributing some kind of power to Shiv that equips him with phenomenal strength that makes him empower us every time. If we have to win against them, then all of them have to be separated,' Aghora said.

'But there is one more mysterious power that is helping them,' Aghora said.

'What kind of mysterious power?' Marich asked.

'That techie guy's brain had memory traces of strange happenings; he had visualised Shiv getting killed by your hands and rest all of them had been captured by you. The fire spirits were confident that what they saw in that techie's brain were not dreams, they were actual events.

Now, I don't really know how and what did he see, but I can certainly tell you that he had a decisive role in Shiv's escape from our trap.

But this is just one aspect. There seems to be a bigger game at play.

Surprisingly, Shiv's brain remembered to have been helped by a strong female power,' Aghora said.

'Female power; what are you talking about?' Marich said.

'Yes, even I was puzzled with it at first and if my guesses are correct then this female power is somehow associated with Naina,' Aghora said.

'Naina! But...but you told me that you have ensured that her soul does not stay in the spirit realm and has crossed over to the other world,' Marich exulted.

'That is what is confusing me. The power I am talking about is not a spirit or a ghost, it is something else that is empowering them. And whatever it is, it seems to be benefitting from the proximity of these six members together. These powers Shiv is showing are not just simple siddhis; he is evolving into something else. Something super - human, and it is that mysterious power that is helping him become that,' Aghora said.

'Then how do we control them?' Marich asked.

'It has to be a multipronged strategy. First, we will have to separate them. Then, we target everything that Shiv aims to protect. And lastly, we fight Shiv's super - human powers by making him fight a super - human from another world,' Aghora said.

Marich's face lit up with the thought of the new sinister plot that played in his mind.' so, the time has come to unleash the monster we have been preparing for so long,' Marich said.

What can be the Map of the Universe? I was deeply contemplating in Shiv's brain. In the human world, map means a paper on which angles, bearings, and distances are represented as representative fractions of actual places as on the surface of Earth. It sounds as if God has left some kind of mathematical formula to find him and humans are unaware of it? Shiv was thinking, I was thinking.

'I got it…I got it…it's 3D!' the sudden announcement by Sarvan disturbed me and Shiv together.

'What's the matter?' Shiv asked. 'What time is it?'

Shiv noticed that Sarvan was grinning from ear to ear. Somehow, Sarvan had started behaving like a lunatic. He was always in an irritatingly happy state. I knew the reason. For a brief moment, Sarvan had experienced the taste of divine blissful energy state and now he longed to be only in that blissful state.

Since I am Consciousness, I need a body or a Sharira to be realised. Now, because a human body cannot travel outside the three dimensions, hence, I use a Sukhshma Sharira or Astral body to travel to dimensions beyond the fourth dimension. The experiences of Sarvan's sukhshma sharira(astral body), when it was free of its bodily constraints and shuttling in the loop of time, were still preserved as a memory inside the physical body and Sarvan had tasted this memory of infinite happiness. He had been hosted to the fact that the treasure of true bliss rests outside the boundaries of the human body. In the human world, people unattached to the material world are considered insane and Sarvan was turning into one. But the condition we were in presently, lunacy seemed most sensible. So, it was important to listen to Sarvan.

'What…what do you mean?' Shiv asked.

'It's 3D!' Sarvan reiterated and forwarded the Shree - Yantra that Shiv used to wear and pointed at the intersection of the geometrical lines.

'Are you mad? It is just an intersection of nine triangles,' Shiv said, looking at the Shree - Yantra.

'Oh! I am sorry. Maybe I am hallucinating. I thought that maybe I saw it as an interaction of nine pyramids,' Sarvan said with a childish smile and turned to go back.

Shiv turned and rested his back against the banyan tree and closed his eyes. After just a few moments of nap, suddenly, Shiv sprang to life as if stung by a scorpion and ran inside. It was now Shiv's turn to get mad.

All the family members were sitting in the hall with Rohan sitting in front of his mother and playing with the Shree - Yantra when Shiv snatched the Yantra from him to take a good look at it.

'Behold! His majesty is here! Can someone tell me why does this guy always makes an entry as if he were a descendent of Thor?' Santy said, casually looking at Shiv.' What is wrong now?' Santy asked.

'It's just that…it's…it's…' Shiv stammered.

'It's 3D,' Sarvan said.

'What! You fucking squinty - eyed lunatic! What is your peanut - sized brain dreaming now?' Santy said sarcastically to Sarvan.

'The Shree - Yantra is not a drawing of triangles' said Sarvan, unmindful of the insult by Santy, 'It is an intersection of cones when seen as a three - dimensional object rather than a two dimensional drawing.'

'If anyone dares to mention the word dimension again, I will bloody castrate him,' Santy said.

'I believe that threat excludes me,' Vani interrupted Santy.' Sarvan is right. The intricate geometry of Shree - Yantra hides many secrets inside it and has been the centre subject of many scientific researches. Shree - Yantra is also used as a 3D object, let me show you on internet,' Vani said and reached for Rohan's laptop kept in the truck which was parked outside the temple.

Moments later the entire gang was looking conspicuously at the laptop which Rohan was now controlling. Vani was sitting next to Rohan with her left hand over his right shoulder and the rest of the members stood all around them. Everyone stood there, except Santy, who was now happily feasting on breakfast. All the members present there had realised that a hungry Santy could be troublesome.

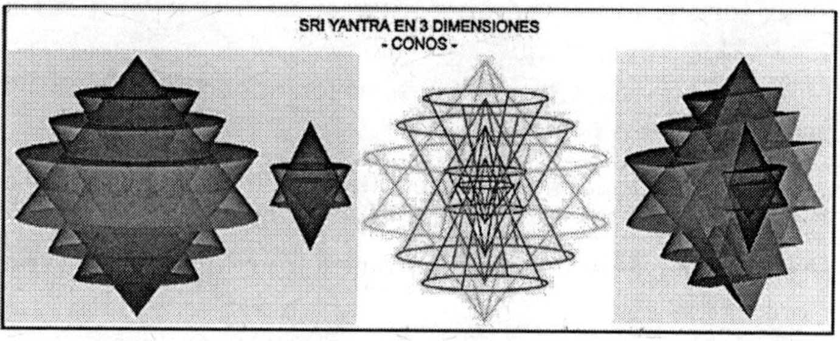

After a few hours of pondering over several sites and articles, Vani finally began to explain.' Mathematics, as they say, is the language in which the universe was created.

The most glaring example of universal geometry is the divine proportion or the Golden Ratio as some call it. This ratio is also known as 'Phi' and its numerical value upto three digits is 1. 618; of course, the ratio extends upto infinity. Everything that exists in nature is constructed in a proportionally precise manner to this proportion called the Golden/Phi Ratio.

It is a simple mathematical relationship found naturally and in many great works of art (Leonardo Da Vinci's Vitruvian man and the Mona Lisa) and even architecture such as the positioning of the pyramids of Giza.

The beauty of someone's face is also based upon this golden proportion. Apple Company uses the principle of golden proportion to design their products to make them more appealing to the customer's eye. Our bodies are also designed on this golden proportion.

In simple terms, the golden ratio suggests that everything, starting from the tiniest speck, expands and grows in proportions of 1. 618, from a microscopic level to a macroscopic level for increased stability and beauty. Famous mathematician Pythagoras said that the golden ratio is the blueprint applied to all of creation.

Another series called the Fibonacci series is also a representation of the golden proportion. The mathematics of the golden ratio and of the Fibonacci sequence is intimately interconnected. The Fibonacci series is formed by summing up the two predecessor numbers.

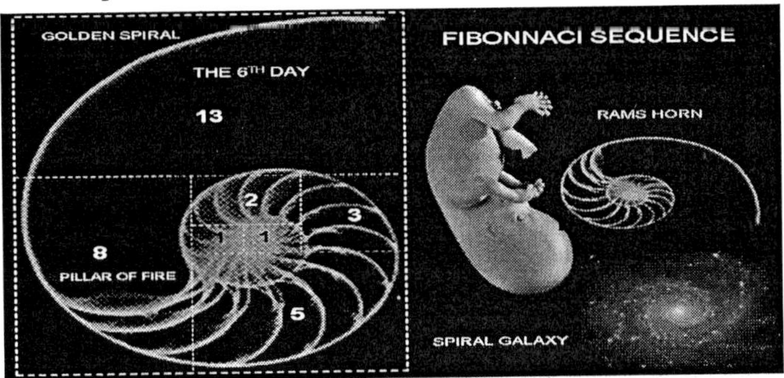

The Fibonacci sequence is: 1, 1, 2, 3, 5, 8, 13, 21, 34, 55, 89, 144, 233, 377, 610, 987 and so on. Therefore, if a Fibonacci number is divided by its immediate predecessor in the sequence, the quotient approximates Phiratio; e. g. 987/610 ≈ 1. 6180327868852.

When we draw a spiral based on golden ratio by drawing rectangles repeated within larger golden ratio rectangles, we find that we often see the shape of this spiral in the natural world. The Solar System and the Milky Way galaxy are golden spirals. The diameters of Earth and Moon are also related in the same manner. Even a seashell or a flower grows and gets its design by this very ratio. All human beings and animals invariably follow this ratio between their body parts.

Now, the Shree - Yantra is a mathematically precise design based upon the golden proportion or Phi ratio. Shree - Yantra's are formed by 9 interlocking isosceles triangles. 4 of them point upwards and represent the female energy, Shakti, while the other 5 point downwards, representing the male energy, Shiva.

These triangles are not ordinarily composed but have aspects of the golden ratio in them. Just as we can have rectangles drawn to the specifications of the golden ratio, triangles too can be drawn to have similar properties.

What is most intriguing is that the Shree - Yantra bears a striking similarity with the Star of David and the Flower of Life.' Vani paused for a moment.

'What is the flower of life?' Santy, who was now attentive and listening to the complete monologue, asked.

'Well, Flower of Life is a geometric pattern that has been found to have been worshipped by many civilisations of the past including India.

The earliest cultures including the Christians, Hindus, Greeks, and Egyptians recognized that there were different patterns or geometric shapes that repeated throughout nature. They also worked out that there was a correlation or connection between the various elements found on Earth and the heavens. These connections or common patterns, known as sacred geometry, were mirrored; that is to say,the same patterns appeared on Earth and the sky and were believed by these ancient cultures to exist in all parts of the universe.

They also recognized that these small patterns were representative of the building blocks that were literally the blueprints for everything in the universe. A seed, after all, contains all the material needed to become a mighty tree regardless of the size of the tree. A single cell contains all the elements of the whole body, and the Earth and heavens are reflections of each other. This idea represented by the saying 'As above, so below' summarized this ancient belief.

Scientists now have factually verified that the Flower of Life is the creation pattern of everything in existence, including intangible things like thoughts, dreams, music, and emotions. The Flower of Life contains the exact geometry of the Star of David and the Seed of Life both of which have been widely accepted as the sacred geometry of the universe.

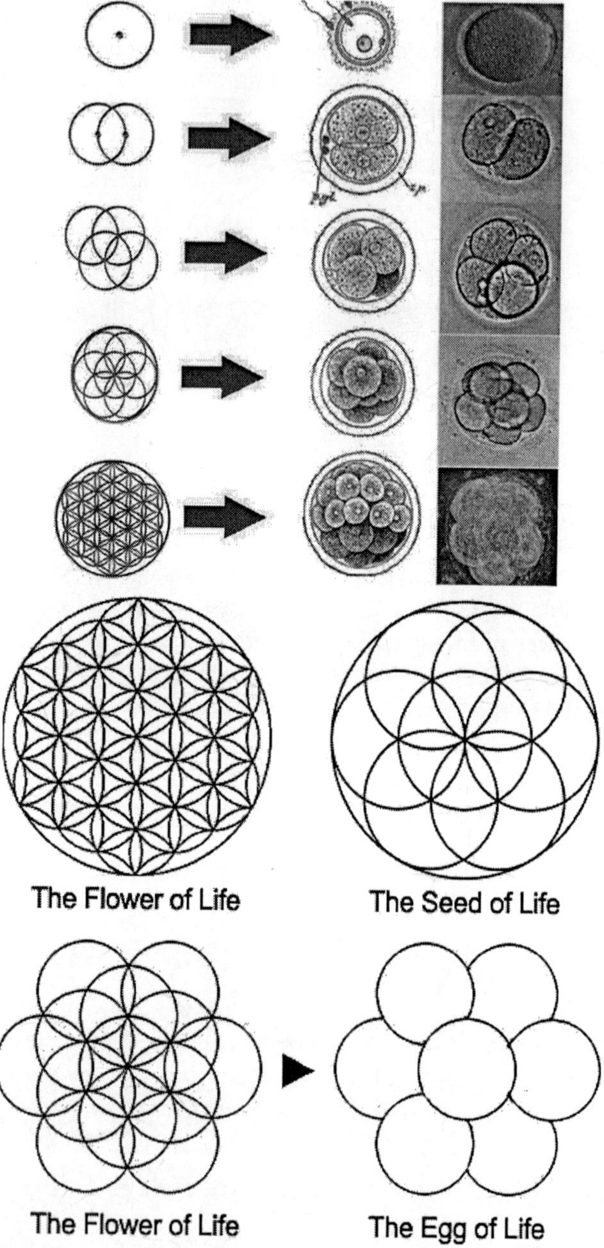
The Flower of Life
The Seed of Life
The Flower of Life
The Egg of Life

Now, if I start explaining the mathematics of these sacred symbols, it will take months to just cover the introduction. So I will straight away jump to the point without complicating things too much.

The bottom line is that the Shree - 'Yantra is a geometrical figure that contains all the secret formulas and equations using which God has created the universe,' Vani said.

'Perhaps, it is much more than that,' Shiv said in a manner that grabbed everyone's attention. Shiv told Rohan to open an internet video that showed the holographic image of Shree - Yantra in its 3D form with cones instead of triangles manifesting the Yantra. As Rohan pressed play, the image started to rotate.

Shiv kept on gazing through the image for some time. Then Shiv told Rohan to again open the 2D image of the Shree - Yantra. For some time, Rohan kept on browsing through the internet as per Shiv's direction.

Shiv asked Rohan to download an image of a human body and overlap the 2D image of the Shree - Yantra over it.

To everyone's surprise, when fit to exact proportions, the apex of the seven central cones exactly coincided with the exact location of the chakras in the human body. The downward - pointing triangles symbolizing female energy coincided with the four lower chakras and the upward - pointing triangles symbolizing male energy coincided with the three upper chakras.

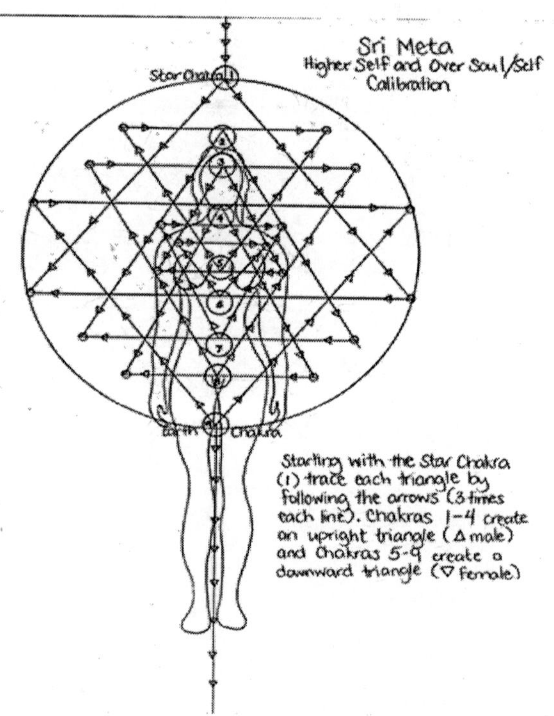

While everyone was surprised, Shiv kept on gazing at the image and absorbed the details.

Next, Shiv told Rohan to download an image of the Flower of

Life and superimpose it upon a 2D image of the Shree - Yantra. The results were again astounding. The circular geometry exactly matched the triangular geometry with the apex of each triangle precisely touching the circumference of a circle with the base of the triangles acting as the diameter of the circle.

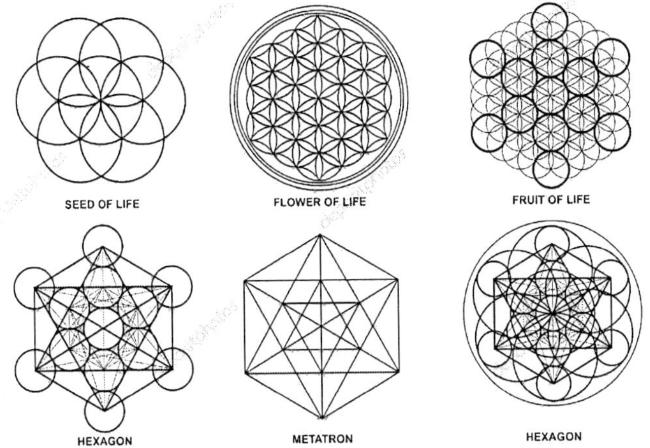

After gazing over the images, Shiv again switched back to the 3D holographic image of Shree - Yantra.

Shiv kept on gazing inside the rotating holographic image for more than an hour. 'It is not just an image,' Shiv finally spoke after considerable pondering. 'It is the Map of the Universe.'

CHAPTER 18

THE VIRTUE OF HUMAN STUPIDITY

As Shiv slept that night, I was awakened to a new reality.

The memories of my last conversation with Chit kept coming back to me.

'The God's dilemma of duality.'

'There is a Map of the Universe.'

'As it is outside, so is it inside.'

'A seeker shall always find God or God will find him.'

God had indeed created a mathematics of the universe to help mankind find him. A map is nothing but a diagrammatic representation of the angles and bearings of the features on the ground on a piece of paper. The answer to the riddle of God was hidden somewhere within the angles and ratios of that incredible geometry called the Shree - Yantra. It was so close and yet so far from me.

But there was another realisation.

Since I was the only one who had travelled through time into a parallel universe; therefore, I alone knew the sinister plan of Marich. For rest of the family members, it was just a day of unusually dangerous happenings that they were undergoing. For Santy to frown upon Rohan or Shiv was not unusual as he hardly knew the dangers that they were in.

Only I knew, and hence, I was the knower of truth. But at

the same time, I was the knower of only partial truth and not the absolute truth because I was the knower of only the truth that was happening in this timeline or maybe this universe. Also, I didn't know why everything was happening this way? For example, I didn't know why Marich was doing what he intended to do or why only these six humans had been caught in this web.

I travelled through the minds of the family members who were sleeping in serene silence. The physical exhaustion imparted by the day's events had sent them into a deep slumber. But even in deep sleep, their minds were active and I could gauge the activities in their minds. Only one mind was relaxed; it was Sarvan's.

Sarvan was most foolish of them all. In fact, he had gone nuts. He had willingly and cheerfully parted away with his wife and now behaved as if he had lost his mental balance, but deep inside, there was a strange calmness in him amidst all this turmoil. It was as if he was untouched by the day's events that had shaken everyone to the core. It was as if he was lost in something beyond the physical reality; something which even I was not able to grasp.

After observing the human world from the eyes of many different personalities and after being a witness to so many twists of different destinies, I am most certain of one fact of life that to be actually happy in this human world, one has to be slightly foolish.

A super - achiever can never be happy throughout his life. The childish innocence and dreamy demeanour are quintessential ingredients for happiness. Anyone who is very meticulous and calculative about his life can never live life to the fullest. Because what is life other than a series of unexpected accidents.

The unforeseen fiascos, the unanticipated glitches, are all that add meaning to life and the indomitable will of human beings to conquer all odds is what fills one's lifetime with memories.

So, while these unpredicted happenings will frustrate an intelligent mind, they will bemuse a foolish mind. While they will induce a fear of helplessness in a calculative mind, they will inflame wonder in a childish mind. Because the so - called unwise never aim to control life. Life is as such out of their control; they merely want to flow along the wake of life while the so - called wise resist the natural flow of life.

Life is a force; an actual physical force in being. And no matter how strong you consider yourself, life will blow you away. You cannot resist or withstand the force of life. So, the best way is to learn to fly in the force of life and never mind its turbulence. It's somewhat similar to the way birds float along the thermals and torrents of air. Birds don't mind if a gust of wind elevates them hundreds of feet up in the sky or brings themcloser to the ground. After all, it is just air, and birds are designed by nature to endure the gushes of air. That's all the fun there is to be a bird.

Mankind is fighting an outrageous war against human stupidity, and I choose to fight on the side of human stupidity because the illusion of human intelligence is far more unwise than human stupidity.

An intelligent human mind would prefer a straight instead of a twisted branch of a tree because they can cut wooden planks out of it which can give flawless shape to a lifeless building; while a stupid mind would stay engrossed at the intricate geometry of the twisted branch admiring its incomprehensible shape. What the intelligent mind has failed to notice is that flowers and fruits grow on such a twisted branch. That twisted shape is also a perfect design of nature, unfathomable to them due to their limited knowledge.

So, if I find a human being who is still twisted in his nature and flawed in his behaviour, I consider my findingsprecious as he is the branch who has not been converted into a dead plank to fit int society. Only such a stupid person can spread life in the form of flowers and spread happiness in the form of selfless contribution to society. Life will grow on that person.

Sarvan was one such find. Being in a dreamy state,while everyone's mind wandered into unknown dimensions; Sarvan's mind had a strange stillness in it as if somehow all his thoughts were merging and vanishing into nothingness.

Vani woke up in the middle of the night as if disturbed by a bad dream. The darkness inside the temple was only partially lit by the moonlight of the full moon entering through the small windows in the temple walls.

She composed herself and looked at Rohan's mother's face sleeping next to her. She got up to move out of the temple door for a breath of fresh air.

While she was moving out, her foot hit someone. There she saw Sarvan sleeping like a child under the main idol in a blissfully deep slumber. Vani sat next to him and gazed at his dimly lit face in the moonlight. Despite years of estranged relationship, there was a bond that connected her to Sarvan. There was a part of her life that she had spent with him that was difficult to forego.

She lay down next to Sarvan facing him and put her arm around his. Sarvan was unaware of all of this as if he was not present in his body at that time.

As Vani gazed at his face, memories of all the time they had spent with each other kept coming back to her. She felt as if the events of the last few days had never occurred.

They could have had a beautiful relationship. For so many years she had longed for his love which he never expressed. And today, the same man was lying before her, vulnerable like a child. Sarvan had completely lost his serious software engineer demeanour and seemed to have become carefree and mentally imbalanced. Somewhere deep inside her heart, there were fond memories of her husband.

She loved him. Vani went closer to Sarvan's face till her warm breath gently touched Sarvans lips. Then she drew his face closer and kissed him. Tears rolled down her eyes as she kissed Sarvan. She had yearned for this kiss and waited a long time. All emotions poured out in that one kiss as she held his face in her hands.

Years of unspoken words had coagulated deep inside her as tears, and now, they flooded her face as her lips expressed both their love and anger to the person she had spent a part of her youth with.

It was something more than a kiss. It was a communication which they could never have.

As Vani rested Sarvan's face and turned back, she saw Rohan standing and looking at her.

Rohan sat near Vani, held her hand, and spoke softly, 'I understand Vani…I am never going to…' His sentence was cut short by Vani putting her index finger on Rohan's lips indicating him to stop talking. She was suppressing her tears and kept her palm on Rohan's cheek. Her face had turned pinkish and her eyes droopy, it was best to leave this moment unsaid.

She motioned Rohan to lie down next to her. Rohan lay down beside her. Without speaking another word, Vani turned her face away to wrap Rohan's arm around her waist and cuddled his body around hers.

Rohan embraced her body in a tight hug as if reassuring her about his love for her. He pressed his face into the fragrance of her hair and planted a kiss from behind her at the junction of her neck and shoulder. Vani, Rohan, and Sarvan slept next to each other hugging each other in a strange new relationship that they had interwoven themselves into.

CHAPTER 19

THE FIGHT BETWEEN GOOD AND EVIL

On the full moon night, in a forlorn farmhouse located amidst the isolation of the jungle on a hilltop, there was huge vessel kept on the giant balcony which was filled with blood up to the brim. As Aghora looked on, Marich emerged from within the vessel drenched in blood. Marich was stark naked with the dripping blood silhouetting his nakedness in the moonlight.

Aghora moved around Marich, observing him from head to toe and from front to behind. Even in his sixties, Marich had the body of a teenager. Years of Ayurvedic medication had restored the youth of Marich and he looked chiselled in his ultra - muscular frame.

'You are ready,' Aghora said, after a detailed inspection of Marich's blood - soaked body. Then in the most commanding voice, he stated,' Now is the time to make the decision. Are you ready to know the secret of the world we live in? The secret will change you forever, it will take away whatever human element you have left in you,but at the same time, it will make you the strongest ruler the modern world has ever seen. It will grant you powers beyond imagination. But first you will have to willingly express your desire for that. Are you ready, Marich?'

'Yes, I am ready,' Marich shouted.

'Then first accept me as your guru. Say it,' Aghora continued in his commanding tone.

Marich bowed to Aghora as a mark of gratitude and said,' O

knower of the deepest secrets; O master of tantric powers, I accept you as my guru, Aghora.'

Aghora's chest swelled and his eyes reflected a fiery shadow.' then I accept you as my most worthy disciple, and now, I am going to tell you the deepest secret of the modern world. Whatever I am going to tell you now, believe every word of it because very few in this world will have access to this profound knowledge.'

Aghora made Marich sit on the ground in the same naked state and sat opposite him and started the narration.

'In modern times, mankind has been conditioned to believe that their lives revolve around economy, democracy, and science; however, it is just eyewash.

In fact, since the time mankind has come into existence, it has been driven in accordance with the laws dictated by higher beings. You can call them aliens or Gods or celestial beings as you may like but the truth is that mankind has forever been in a tussle with each other as per the desire of these beings,' Marich said.

'Then why don't we know about them?' Marich asked.

'It is because, in modern times, our brains have been reduced in capacity and dimension so that we are unable to see or acknowledge their presence around us. We are now a carbon form of life and restricted to our carbon bodies and these beings exist in an energy form at a frequency and wavelength that our brains cannot perceive.

For example, our visible spectrum is very narrow, so anything outside that visible spectrum cannot be perceived by eyes. Similarly for all our sensory organs. Have you ever wondered why dogs or cats cry at night? It is because they can see the spirits that humans cannot see.

That is why this modern age is characterised by two distinctive features - ignorance and deception, and both these attributes are complementary to each other.

But there have been humans who were able to enhance their

brain capacity and dimension to understand these beings and they documented their experiences. These books are what we call religious texts. To decipher the true knowledge of these scriptures, we need to understand the genesis of duality.

The story of human creationstarted when Rishi Kashyap married many daughters of Daksha Prajapati and with each daughter, a different race was born. Among all the races,the two most important were Devas and Asuras.

From Aditi, Devas were born and from Diti, Asuras were born. Logically speaking, they were brother races born out of the same father. But in reality, they formed a duality opposite of each other.

In a way, they were just two forces of nature in constant struggle with each other. Devas live in the seven upper worlds and Asuras live in the six lower worlds. Mind you, these were all celestial beings. I am talking about a time when present - day humans had not yet come into existence.

Maharishi Bhrigu's son, Shukracharya, was the guru of the Asuras and Maharishi Angira's son, Brihaspathi, was the guru of the Devas.

The eternal fight between Devas and Asuras probably started when Indra (God of Thunder), who was the deity of Devas, gained prominence over Varuna (God of Water), who was revered by Asuras. As the eras passed, the war continued through different yugas with different avatars of God's fighting against different Asuras.

Finally, Lord Vishnu decided to be born as Lord Krishna to put an end to this turmoil by wiping out both Devas and Asuras along with their supernatural powers from the face of Earth to open the path for the last yuga called Kaliyuga to advent on Earth. The war of Mahabharata wiped out the races of both Devas and Asuras from Earth.

After the war of Mahabharata,the Devas with their deity as Indra, settled on the eastern side of Sindhu River forming the Vedic civilisation, and the Asuras settled on the western side of Sindhu River forming the Western civilisation.

It would be pertinent to state here that neither the Devas nor the Asuras were Gods, they were celestial beings with incredible powers derived from being close to God, but you can call them' Demigods'. By this period of time, there was a third entity that had come into being–Humans. Humans were a famished, ignorant, malnourished, and distorted image of the demigods.

It was the period when humans lived in caves and were mesmerised by the sightings of these celestial beings. In the absence of a proper language, humans drew whatever image of Devas or Asuras they saw in their respective regions. The influence of these demigods in different regions led to the start of paganism wherein humans started worshipping these celestial beings by making their idols.

Everything depended upon which part of the world was influenced by which demigod. These demigods acquired the status of kings and queens in their regions. Humans prayed to these demigods and the demigods in turn fulfilled small wishes of human beings from their powers, and so the cycle started.

It wasnot strange that despite being completely distinct and isolated cultures, the Greek Gods very closely resemble Hindu Gods mentioned in scriptures.

Maharishi Brihaspati is Jupiter and closely resembles Thor; Thursday is (Thor's day) also named as Guruvar or Brihaspativar. Greek's Kronos (father of gods and Titans) resembles Maharishi Kashyap (the father of Devas and Asuras). Hera is Goddess Lakshmi (wealth), Athena is Goddess Saraswati (learning and fine arts), Hades is Yamraj (God of Death), Poseidon is God Varuna, and Lord Murugan is Ares (God of War).

The similarities between ancient Hindu and Egyptian Gods are even more strikingly similar. [1]

The chief deity of the Egyptian Empire, **Amun**, was always

1 Source : http://sanatanadham. blogspot. com/2017/01/worship - of - hindu - gods - in - ancient - egypt. html

depicted in temple inscriptions with a blue skin colour and having two feathers in his head - dress. As we know, Krishna's complexion is dark blue and his throne is always decorated with some peacock feathers. **Mut** is described as *the* Queen of the Goddesses, Lady of Heaven, Mother of the Gods, and She Who Gives Birth. She is depicted as having crook and flail (nekhakha) in her hand which originally represents Trishula and Parashu in the hands of Durga.

Khonsu is the originator of the moon and represents solace and satisfaction. He is depicted with heka in his hands which represents a plough. Balarama is also shown as white as the summer cloud. **Atum** has similar attributes to Lord Shiva. Atum carries a staff surmounted by human head wearing a disc. Shiva always wears a garland of skulls around his neck and holds a trident. Just like Atum, he is also a destroyer demigod.

Brahma is mentioned in ancient Egypt as God **Ptah** transliterated from the Sanskrit word 'Pitah' meaning father. Brahma is described as Pitamah(forefather) and Pitah(father) of the universe. Ptah is often depicted on the lotus flower. Brahma is also always shown on the lotus flower. He creates the universe and the beings within this universe.

Babi, also **baba**, in ancient Egypt, was the monkey God. His name literally means the chief of the monkeys or baboons. He fought with the Sun God, Ra. He dances when he hears auspicious music and bestows his mercy. Hanuman tried to eat the Sun mistaking it to be a ripened fruit and thus, had a fight with the Indian Sun God. He chants the name of God in very auspicious sound and dances joyfully.

With the advent of Judaism, Christianity, and Islam,there were two more events that had taken place which would change the course of humanity forever.

Firstly, the advent of Kaliyuga had brought a clout of ignorance and deception upon mankind that had made them forget all the knowledge and even their touch with the remaining demigods was lost. This had started to alter their understanding of God itself.

Second and more importantly, one of the angels of Godhad rebelled against him and chosen to bring suffering to mankind. The name of the angel was Lucifer or Satanin Christianity, Dajjal in Islam, and demon Kali (different from Goddess Kali) in Hinduism.

The powers of Lucifer were no match to the power of God, so he could not directly challenge God and moreover, since both Devas and Asuras were celestial beings, Lucifer could not affect them. So he chose the path of deceiving human beings into believing a false truth to divert them away from the path of God. So, there was further increase in ignorance and deception.

People have forgotten their purpose of life in the modern age and their conflicts are driving the world to extinction. But what humans fail to realise is that both ignorance and deception are malice which have to be dealt with within one's own brain. The conflict in the modern age is internal and not external.' Aghora paused for a while as if giving time to Marich to assimilate what he had spoken till now.

'I can indeed correlate everything now. But guruji, I fail to realise why are you telling me all this now? I am aware of the destructive mentality of humans and that is why I have been working on plans to enslave them by destroying their pineal glands,' Marich said.

Aghora pondered for a while and said, 'Enslaving human beings will give you power, but power is not an end in itself. It is just a means to an end. It is what you do with that power that matters. The time has come for you to realise who you truly are.'

'Who am I? What do you mean? Is there some other secret to my existence?' Marich asked.

'There are more secrets in this world than you can imagine, Marich. With the advent of modern age, most Devas and Asuras returned to their Immortal realms. But all of them did not return; a few decided to stay back disguised as human beings in this mad world designed by human beings.

One such race of Asuras was called Nivata - Kavacha. They were masters of science and technology and had supernatural knowledge of mystical magic. They used to live in floating cities over the ocean and also under it. They were so strong that even the greatest demon king Ravana could not defeat them. They were finally vanquished by Arjun on request of Lord Indra with the help of Rudra weapon after the battle of Mahabharata. With them, the highly sophisticated submarine warfare and flying airships technology was lost.' Aghora again stopped as if lost in some thought.

'Do you mean to say that some of Nivat - Kavacha are still alive?' Marich asked.

'Yes, you and me are the last of Nivat - Kavacha left in this world,' Aghora said.

'WHAT! I belong to the race of Asuras?' Marich exclaimed in wonder.

'That is the truth, Marich, and I have watched over you for my entire life. That is why you are taller and stronger than normal humans. The actions of Lucifer has confused mankind and they are now so much under its spell that they cannot distinguish truth from false. This provides us with the opportunity to bring the reign of Asuras back on Earth, and this time, Devas can do nothing to stop us.

Once we have destroyed the pineal gland in humans, they will not be able to receive any more revelations and all their remaining links with God will be severed. Then with the help of our drugs, we can chemically control them and turn them against the Devas. Mankind will worship only Asuras.

We already control the six Lower Worlds under us. After gaining control of this seventh human world, the balance will tilt in our favour and we will rule over the complete creation.

Mankind will be used as fodder in this magnanimous task to weaken the power of Devas.

Once all mankind thinks alike and worships us, the energy generated by the power of their thoughts and prayers will make us very strong. Then we can re - establish the rule of Asuras back on Earth.' Aghora was speaking as if possessed by some kind of power.

'But what about Shiv?' Marich said.

'Yes Shiv, I always knew he could trouble us because by birth, he is half Asura and half Deva,' Aghora said.

'What! That means, that means...' Marich was short of words for a moment.

'Yes, Naina was a Deva. I realised it when despite my numerous tantrik attempts, I could not kill the baby in her womb. Even as a baby, Shiv just digested every poison that I gave him.

But later due to his disability, I thought of keeping him alive for the simple reason that I wanted to invent a drug that could destroy the pineal gland of Devas.

Think about it, Marich. Had I succeeded and severed the connection of Devas with God, they would have lost all their powers because God is the one who is the source of all their powers.

However, now I feel that keeping that boy alive was a mistake.

Last time when I saw Shiv growing in size and growing extra arms, I knew Devas were helping him. That is why I preferred to move from there.

That is why, this time I have planned to do something that will be beyond the capability of Shiv,' Aghora said.

'If Devas are helping Shiv, then what can be beyond his capability?' Marich asked.

'Shukracharya...I have worshipped him for 33 years and finally, he has answered. This time, the Nags, the disciples guru of Asuras, Maharishi Shukracharya will assist us in our fight,' Aghora said with a twinkle in his eyes.

CHAPTER 20

THE HIDDEN MESSAGE

Next morning, all the family members moved out of the temple and journeyed back towards Goa. The decision was unanimously taken after Rohan declared, 'If the next fight is imminent, we will fight on familiar territory.'

Goa was home. It was the jungle where Rohan had sprawled throughout his childhood. He preferred to tame the wild in the jungle of his choice.

On their way back, Santy picked a newspaper and his eyes got fixed to a catchy news piece that said: -

'The culprits of cannibalism are depicting a zombie like behaviour and are driven by only primary needs like hunger and thirst.'

'Holy Shit! Cannibalism! What are human beings turning into! Just listen to this article, guys.' And Santy read out the article for everyone. Shiv, Rohan, and Sarvan turned at the same time to stare at Santy in disbelief.

Shiv snatched the newspaper from Santy and read it again. In the next one hour of drive,Vani had Googled the complete story of human cannibalism that had turned a marriage ceremony into a gory blood spatter and left 213 dead and 93 injured. All the 61 survivors had gone mad and were presently being investigated in police custody.

'I think there is something that I must tell all of you,' Shiv Said.

'Start from how you grew big and how you grew arms,' Santy said in a sarcastic tone.

'No, it is serious Santy. We must all know what this "inner voice" has been telling me all along,' Shiv said.

'Inner voice?' Santy said. 'Is this guy even normal?'

'I too feel it,' Sarvan butted in with a smile.

'Santy, let's listen to him. Even I feel that there is some intuition guiding me that I am not able to comprehend,' Rohan objected.

'O Hello! Mr Gautam Buddha is also speaking,' Santy said, looking at Rohan. 'I always did doubt that you three have gone nuts. Today you guys have proved me right. Go ahead, I have to tolerate as I cannot jump out of the car but I will troll you till I die due to this and after I die, I will haunt you as a ghost for sharing your inner voice bullshit with me. Go on, shoot.' Santy sounded frustrated.

The rest of the backward journey passed with Shiv narrating incidents that had been stored in his subconscious mind. After a long time, Sarvan became interested and contributed to the discussion by sharing his déjà vu feeling with all the episodes that Shiv shared.

Rohan was also particularly surprised when Shiv narrated incidents that had never taken place but somehow he remembered them happening. The surprising factor was that Rohan also remembered them happening exactly the same way.

Vani was particularly shocked when Shiv told her about the strange connection wherein he felt as if his mother, Naina, somehow connected with him during the last fight and narrated her life story to him after guiding him to victory against Marich.

Vani believed him because from when she had first seen Shiv, she felt a deep unexplained intimacy which she had never felt with any other stranger. She could now understand Shiv's behaviour when he touched her feet after the last fight against Marich.

The rest of the travellers did not utter a single word throughout the rest of the journey. It was too difficult for them to believe everything that was narrated but so was everything that had occurred in front of their eyes since the last few days.

As for me, it was a strange feeling. I was the one narrating the happenings from Shiv's mouth and on the other end, I was the one listening and reacting to the incidents I already knew. I was the one who truly knew what had happened because for me, it was real, not a figment of some imagination or a whisper frommy inner voice. What seemed to be coincidence to these humans was a result of my plans and actions. Weather it was Rohan's untimely rescue of Shiv during his unplanned visit to Shimla or Shiv's discovery about his connection with Vani.

'It's all Karma,' Rohan's mother finally spoke. 'It is written in Bhagwad Gita that all the people who you meet in your lifetime have a Karmic connection between them. Maybe you guys have a Karmic connection between you. Maybe your destinies are connected. Maybe you guys have been brought together by fate to serve a higher purpose.'

'I have a very bad feeling about all this,' Santy said,' those guys are upto something very nasty and somehow we have got ourselves involved in all of this. If they strike again, our best hope of survival against them will be Shiv if he again adorns his Durga Mata form. And the funny thing is even he doesn't know exactly how it happened.'

'Incorrect,' Rohan's mother said.' Your best hope against even the most formidable enemy is faith in God. I don't know how powerful or how many your enemies are, but one thing that I can say with conviction is that Lord Krishna is with you. So victory will be yours.'

'Who is Lord Krishna?' Shiv asked.

'Rohan's mother smiled at Shiv's ignorance.' Come, let me show you,' she said and took everyone inside the puja room.

'Pay your reverence to God's first children; it is because of them that we all are safe in such a difficult time,' Rohan's mother said.

The puja room was full of different types of images of all different Gods.

'You told me na that your inner voice tells you to search for

God. There he is, that is Lord Krishna, have a look at God,' Rohan's mother said.

Rohan's mother pointed towards an image depicting a war scene with two huge armies standing opposite one other and in the middle was a chariot of five white horses whose reins were held by a bluish Godly looking man with a peacock feather on the crown he was wearing. He seemed to be the charioteer. There appeared to be a warrior king standing inside the chariot with inquisitive expressions on his face. On top of the chariot, a monkey God was sitting near a saffron flag which was marked with a fire symbol. There was also a small superimposed image at the corner of the pic wherein there was a young man with seemingly divine vision who was narrating the war to a blind king.

'Here is Shree Krishna as the charioteer,' Rohan's mother went on. 'It is the battleground of Kurukshetra in the epic Mahabharata where he is teaching the principles of Gita to Arjuna; and in a corner, Vidur with his divine vision is narrating the whole scene to the blind king, Dhrithrashtra.'

By now I had understood one thing–all the secrets of the human world lie deep within these tales that have been woven around them. Maybe the earlier human beings were wise enough to understand that if they convert knowledge to science and mathematics it will not last long as very few people will ever read them. However, if they convert knowledge in the form of stories, it will transcend down to thousands of years. The common man can enjoy them as stories while the wise may uncover the deep secrets that lay within the innocent layers of these stories.

'Aunty, if you think Krishna is God,' Shiv said to Rohan's mother,' then I would like to know every story related to Lord Krishna from you.'

Rohan's mother smiled at Shiv's request and said, 'I am happy to know that you want to learn about Lord Krishna. Now - a - days, no kid wants to hear stories. They just want to play on their mobile. But if I will teach you about Lord Krishna, you will first have to accept me as your guru.'

'Guru...What is that?' Shiv inquired.

'The ancient Indian system of teaching advocated Shruti (which has to be heard) and Smriti (which can be remembered) as two ways of learning.

They believed that propagation of knowledge can only be done by a guru to a disciple, who becomes a mentor to the disciple and guides him to the true path of Godly wisdom. So, knowledge was imparted from person to person for centuries until finally, books were written. So, if I will impart you all the knowledge that I have learnt from my grandparents, you have to accept me as your guru,' Rohan's mother said.

'Ok, then I accept you as my guru. Please help me decipher the mystery of God,' Shiv stated.

'There is something strange in this piece of news.' Rohan suddenly came barging into the puja room. 'I googled every detail of this case; these culprits of cannibalism were very normal people who were just attending a marriage ceremony. How can they suddenly turn into savages? There is something fishy and I have an intuition that this incident has some connection with Marich.'

'You have an intuition! Do you have any better clue to support your claim on this subject?' Santy said.

'Last time I believed my intuition, I found Shiv. You will have to trust me this time also,' Rohan pleaded to Santy.

'Boss, what do you think you are: Superman or Spiderman? Even if you are correct, we cannot go after someone like Marich on our own,' Santy said.

'You are right and so we will not go after Marich. We will just go to the mental asylum where the victims of this tragedy have been kept, as only they can tell us exactly what happened that day,' Rohan said.

'We may have to split into two groups,' Shiv said.' While you guys inquire whatever trace you can find about Marich, me and Sarvan will stay here and learn from aunty because my intuition says our pursuit of God is what has kept us alive through all this. I need to learn everything I can from aunty to be prepared to meet Marich next time.'

'Done,' Rohan said. 'I, Vani, and Santy will pursue the case, and you and Sarvan be here and find God or whatever.'

'Wait…Wait... Brother Rohan, why have you nominated me against my wish to go after a dreaded criminal? I want to be in the team which is trying to find God…I…I also want to find God,' Santy raised a concern.

'You cannot be in that team, Santy, as you lack the basic qualifications required for finding God. You will scare God away. As for the reason for being in my team, you are my lucky charm.' Rohan winked at Santy and took him along.

For the next whole month that Rohan, Vani, and Santy were out, Shiv and Sarvan kept on listening to the stories about Lord Krishna throughout the day and kept on reading Bhagwat Gita.

Everyday Rohan's mother would tell them a new story and then they would sit for hours discussing the meaning of the story. Sarvan had the added advantage of internet which he used widely to learn the intricacies of everything they learnt from Rohan's mother.

One thing I learnt was that every single item depicted in these pictures had a deep symbolic meaning behind it. If we take the Kurushetra picture of Lord Krishna, it can be deciphered to have a deep context in the present day.

The chariot is symbolic for the human body and the five horses stand for the five senses which drive the human body. These senses tend to run free and uncontrolled and that is why they have been depicted as horses. The reins are the brain which is used to control these senses to direct them towards the path a person wants to follow. Krishna as the charioteer depicts the power which controls your destiny and Arjun stands for the Soul who is always confused about its real purpose in this world and seeks guidance from God.

The other two characters of the pic also have deep symbolism in the present day context. Vidur stands for a guru who is enlightened enough to see and understand the true interaction between God and a Soul, and the blind king, Dhritrashtra,is symbolic for the state in which humans are today who despite being guided by a guru will still not understand the difference between good and bad as they are intermingled in the web of their own ego and nature. Despite fully knowing that the war would lead to an end of the clan, Dhritrashtra still could not give up his ego and greed.

The armies depicted in the battle scene also symbolically represent the constant struggle between good and bad that takes place in our mind.

Rohan's mother told Shiv about other stories from the life of Lord Krishna. The time Shiv spent with Rohan's mother were his best moments ever lived. For the first time in his life, he had a mother. He loved the care and loved her in return. He would stand alongside her while she cooked food, and pressed her feet when she slept.

During that short time, he had developed a stronger mother - son bond than the guru - disciple bond. Rohan's mother was a source of strength for Shiv; she loved him like her real son.

One day Rohan's mother showed a beautiful blueish stone to Shiv.' this stone is Neelum (blue sapphire). It is very powerful, it had stayed in our family for generations but somehow it didn't suit anyone in my family. Maybe it was waiting for you.

Among all the nine astrological gemstones, the Neelum (blue sapphire) is the strongest and fastest acting gemstone. It is governed by the planet Saturn, which is a planet that has the power to exalt a person to great heights and also,can act negatively and bring tremendous misfortune.

Neelum gives its wearer mental clarity and clears confusion and doubts. Therefore, an individual wearing a blue sapphire can take the right decision even amidst multiple reasons of confusion surrounding the situation. It also helps in improving focus and concentration. It balances the Crown Chakra, thereby resulting in the balance of the cosmic energies in the human body.

Rohan's mother had got a three - dimensional structure of Shree - Yantra and got the Neelum fixed right in its centre. She had got cloth bands fixed to the sides so that it could be easily worn around one's forehead. Rohan's mother tied it around Shiv's head. Immediately, I felt a sensational new energy entering into Shiv's brain which enhanced my powers. The Shree - Yantra had become majestic.

Sarvan, on the other hand, had started spending most of his time at the beach, either meditating or simply watching the ocean. He remained quiet most of the time and whenever he spoke, he spoke with childlike enthusiasm. Sarvan looked happy as if he had completely forgotten about his job and past life. He had discovered some source of happiness inside himself, something that was keeping him continuously radiant.

As much as I try to uncover the secret of human life, one thing remains certain. The secret of human happiness lies deep inside human beings themselves. It is futile to search for happiness outside. No other human being, howsoever dear, will give you everlasting happiness. No material possession, howsoever great, will last a lifetime. No glory, howsoever farfetched, will keep you elevated forever.

Real happiness comes from discovering oneself. It is a law of nature. It created everything unique, so that everything strives to be the best version of itself and every single being departs with his own unique experience of life.

Nature gives you birth fully equipped with everything to experience life to the fullest and to enjoy all its bliss. It is all crammed together in this package called the human body; all sources of joy, all emotions, all knowledge are inside one's own body. Everything has been endowed upon human beings as a part of Godly inheritance.

It is like being born into a wealthy family. If you can learn to enjoy within the possessions of your family, you will never feel wanting. However, if you are jealous of what your neighbours are holding, you will be sad forever.

Humans must exploit the gifts that God has endowed upon them without comparing their gifts with some other person. They will be happiest if they just consider that they have the best gift of God. After all, their gift was designed keeping their uniqueness in mind.

CHAPTER 21

THE FINAL QUEST

Rohan, Vani, and Santy had undertaken the first detective mission of their lives and it was turning into the worst decision they had taken either collectively or individually. Weeks of investigative efforts to the cause of cannibalism had led to nothing.

The culprits of the cannibalism disaster were all kept in different mental hospitals of the country. The detective trio went everywhere only to get the same shocked and blank look from every single culprit.

It was frustrating. Despite being in different parts of the country, 59 survivors spoke exactly the same version as if they were totally oblivious to the happenings on the day the massacre happened. It was as if they were possessed by some kind of power.

It had already been 21 days since they had left Goa and they were running out of patience. They were chasing a mirage.

Their last destination was a small Government - owned mental hospital in Thane, in the suburbs of Mumbai. Only two last culprits were kept in that rickety place.

There was only one thing different.

The two were not part of the marriage ceremony. They were the guards of the venue where the marriage ceremony was held.

'What surprises me,' Rohan said, after speaking to them, 'is that why on Earth would the guards of the venue get drawn into the bloodbath? Why didn't they just run away?'

'There was something that happened which we are not able to catch. Something mysterious,' Vani remarked.

'These narrations are so similar that when they were exhausted after their blood feast, they all complained of a headache at the same place. I get a headache out of hunger and they out of overeating,' Santy said.

The trio had started to walk out of the mental asylum when a thought struck Rohan.

'But of course! Santy, you are a genius! There was something in their head,' Rohan exclaimed and ran to the doctor.

When the reports of the CT scan arrived, they were all normal.

Rohan was booking a taxi back to Goa when he got the report that one of the culprits in Thane's mental asylum had committed suicide by cutting his veins. The reason quoted by the hospital authorities was deep depression.

'There is one last hope,' Vani said.' Before we leave, let's do one thing. Let's post - mortem the brain of this dead culprit.'

'She is right, the body might still be in mortuary. I can dig it out with just a bottle of rum,' Santy said.

'But who will do the post - mortem?' Vani asked.

'I have a plan,' Santy said smiling.

That night, they went as per Santy's plan.

The trio kidnapped a brain surgeon when he was moving out after his night shift and then smuggled the body of the dead culprit from the mortuary after bribing the guard with liquor. Then they stole a hospital ambulance and forced the doctor to perform an autopsy on the body inside the ambulance.

At least Santy was happy with the execution of his plan.

Thankfully, the doctor was sane. He understood the desperation of these strangers and did the autopsy devotedly.

'I have been following this case in the newspapers and was intrigued by its complicacy,' the doctor said after the examination, 'and I am ready to forgive you guys only because the results are startling. This guy has a fully calcinated pineal gland. Normally, partial calcination occurs by middle age but here in this dead body, the gland has totally turned into a rock.'

The doctor pointed to a pea - sized gland located right in the centre of the brain.' this can totally destroy the sleep cycle of the victim and reduce their life span. What is worse is that they will be devoid of human imagination and they will live like a zombie.

So this can explain their current behaviour, although I am not sure if this would lead to cannibalism. I have a few contacts who can help me find it,' the doctor said.

'Who?' Santy asked out of curiosity.

'Mr. Natraj, the owner of Tripura Pharmaceuticals Pvt Ltd. They are the leading drug manufacturers in this country. His company is the main supplier of medicines to my hospital also. He has been in this business for some thirty years and knows everything there is to know about chemicals. I have met him many times for business reasons. Maybe he can tell me what kind of chemical can cause full calcination of a human'spineal gland,' said the doctor, while wiping his specks.

The trio spent the night thanking the doctor, returning the dead body and the ambulance.

After twenty - four days of continuous slogging, they had found a lead. They slept well that night.

The next morning, that doctor was found deadin his house. Preliminary inspection suggested a heart attack due to drug overdose.

'I cannot believe this,' Santy said.' the doctor was perfectly hale and hearty last night when we had dropped him to his house.'

'Last night he spoke about some Mr. Natraj from Tripura Pharmaceuticals Pvt Ltd, I have googled it. Their main office is in Bandra,' Vani said.

CHAPTER 22

THE GURU's WISDOM

Tripura Pharmaceuticals Pvt Ltd. had a huge skyscraper for the main office complex at the suburb of Bandra overlooking the coastline. When Rohan, Vani, and Santy entered the complex, they were overwhelmed by its majestic magnificence, the shining white floor, and a glittering chandelier adorning the intricately designed architectural wonder.

At the centre of the main hall,a huge portrait of Marich was hanging.

'It's the same guy Shiv was fighting. He seems to be the owner of this place,' Rohan said.

'We need to find out what exactly is this guy up to,' Vani said.

Santy went to the reception counter. 'Excuse me! We are here to see that guy on that big billboard. Can you ask him to come down or do you want us to go up?' Santy asked the person atthe reception centre.

The guy looked at Santy from head to toe and said, 'sir, I have been serving here for nine years and have never had a visitor for Mr. Marich Natraj. He doesn't like to meet people.'

Santy went back to Rohan and Vani. 'Breaking news! The name of that person is Marich Natraj. I am pretty sure it is the same Mr. Natraj that doctor wanted to meet before he died.'

'This might be the same Marich we are looking for, the guy is a nasty one for sure,' Vani said.' But do you guys feel that the massacre at the marriage ceremony, the death of the doctor etc. can be related to him.'

'We will need to find that out,' Rohan said.' Let us sneak into his office.'

The trio sneaked in and took the service elevator till the 28th floor, then they took the staircase till the next floor. As they wandered around the next floor, they noticed that all the doors had a biometric entrance system which was impossible to bypass.

'Who is there?'they were startled by the call of a security guard that challenged them from the end of the corridor.

'We have been called to repair the computer malfunction in Mr. Marich's office. We are looking for our way to his office,' Santy lied instinctively.

'Identification Code please,' the guard said, pointing a gun towards them.

For a moment,the barrel of the gun facing them sent Shivers down their spine.

'Here it is,' Santy fibbed again, taking out a piece of card from his pocket.

The guard hesitated for a moment and came close to them. 'Have you not been given the Identification Code?' the guard called again.

'Well, they said "Show this to the guards and they will let you go. It is signed by Mr Marich himself"', Santy replied.

The guard came closer and slung arm his rifle to have a look at the card Santy was holding. It was a card for Shoppers Stop special discount.

'You bastards!' The guard cried and tried to raise his gun. Rohan held the guard and resisted his efforts. In the meantime, Vani inserted an injection in the neck of the guard and he fainted.

Rohan and Santy looked at Vani with surprise.

'I got it from the ambulance' Vani said, looking at their surprised faces. 'It is what they use to make patients subconscious. The doctor told me.'

'You know Vani, your intelligence is more seductive than your beauty,' Santy said,smiling in a flirtatious tone.

Rohan gave an angry stare to Santy and said, 'Let's finish the job at hand.'

The trio dragged the body of the guard till the end of the corridor and pressed his thumb on the scanner. For the next step, a scanner scanned the guard's retina and the door opened.

Inside the door was a huge multi - storeyed laboratory whose levels were visible through glass walls. The entire setup was so highly technologically advanced that it looked surreal. There were hundreds of workers working on all floors.

The building was designed in a way that this central laboratory was invisible to anyone visiting the building. It was cylindrical in shape with the inner stone walls of the cylinder placed right in the centre of the building that made it impossible to ascertain its existence.

From the inside, the cylindrical laboratory was almost completely made up of glass that gave it an imposing look.

At first, the trio were startled by the grand and sophisticated design. As they regained their composure, they headed for the nearest glass door that led them to a circular glass corridor.

There was a strange sense of urgency among the workers in the laboratory. The trio just followed the direction that everyone seemed to be heading to.

At the end of the corridor, there was a huge hall in which three giant screens were placed. There were hundreds of workers gathered there in front of those huge screens.

'Greetings to all the workers of our dream mission,' An announcement echoed through the hall.' together we all had seen a dream to free the world of human deceit and treachery. 'Finally, the day has arrived when this dream will be realised.' the crowd cheered towards a figure who was standing on the window of the top floor just above those screens. 'In sixty seconds from now, the world will change forever. It will be our world. Let the countdown begin.' Amidst the roaring cheer from the crowd, the man's face flashed on the screens. It was Marich.

The screens went blank again and now only the countdown timers flashed reverse counting from 60 seconds. With every passing second, the crowd held their breath and gaped in silence.

When the countdown was over, a missile flashed on each screen, blasting out of their silos and accelerated towards their targets. The scene now showed the targets.

'Oh my God! It looks like Mumbai,' exclaimed Santy.

The missiles exploded few hundred meters above their destined targets over the city of Mumbai, producing a cloud of gas that covered almost the entire city of Mumbai.

'No,' Santy cried.

Suddenly, the three were rendered unconscious by a wave of shock on their necks. The receptionist had apparently tracked the missing guests through the cameras and alerted guards, who had tracked them down till the hall.

When they opened their eyes, it was Déjà vu for Rohan. They were tied motionless in glass pillars in Marich's office on the top floor of the building. Marich was standing in front of them.

'Greetings, old friends' Marich said. 'I applaud your courage to enter my kingdom. You have come at the right time. Get ready to watch the spectacle.'

It was exactly thirty days since Rohan, Vani, and Santy had left Goa.

'Today, I will be giving the final lesson to you,' Rohan's Mother told Shiv and Sarvan. 'I have already told whatever I learnt from my grandparents about God but today, I will talk to both of you separately. First, Shiv will sit with me.'

Rohan's mother took Shiv inside the puja room and closed the door. Then, she made Shiv sit opposite to her.

When they were in a deep meditative state, Rohan's mother spoke gently, 'Close your eyes and concentrate all your attention in the area of the third eye.' Shiv obeyed.

'Now with closed eyes, imagine the reality that we are living in presently. Try to visualise me sitting in front of you and the other objects kept around you in the room. Try to locate as many objects as you can visualise, based on their image in your subconscious mind,' Rohan's mother said.

Shiv visualised the picture of the puja room that he was sitting in, the images of different Gods pasted on the walls, the idols adorned with garlands and glittering cloths and finally, Rohan's mother as his guru who was sitting in front of him.

'Now imagine every single item of the room disappearing in the air with only me remaining in front of you,' Rohan's mother continued.

The meditative practice took Shiv into depths within himself. Every single item they had visualised started disappearing into thin air until there was complete darkness all around with only Rohan's mother sitting in front of him.

Out of all the activities that I have seen humans doing, concentration or meditation is the only one which makes sense to me. The reason for this belief can be attributed to the absurdity of human lifestyle.

All the problems humans face are a creation of their mind, but for some reason, they believe that they can deal with their problems by providing comfort to their bodies instead of directly confronting their minds.

Let us understand it differently. Most of the time humans have very little control over their senses. It is, on the contrary, these senses which drive the human life.

So, when they feel hungry, they eat; when they feel a craving, they indulge; when they feel scared, they hoard material things and feel safe.

The entire human world is designed to first create an illusion of fear and then take measures to overcome it.

I have come to believe that human beings are most scared of two things: the first is nature and the second is they themselves.

When humans are afraid that the weather can harm them, they create houses to create an artificial weather around them. When they feel scared of diseases, they make medicines and purifying devices.

They have also devised a system of law to protect themselves from other humans. In effect, they try to protect themselves from the very things that are designed to protect them.

Nature has designed human body with an ability to adapt to the vagaries of weather and contains immunity to co - exist with millions of microorganisms. Human body has been designed for survival rather than protection.

By shutting the human body away from nature in an artificial environment, humans have curtailed its ability to evolve and overtime, this has made human body weak and vulnerable.

Humans try to overcome this weakness by possessions that can provide them bodily comfort or seemingly secure their future.

In fact, security and possessions are illusions which humans have created for themselves because human body is just a protective cover given for a short duration on Earth in which a person can explore his mind. Their real purpose is to understand Me. A house full of belongings cannot substitute a mind full of stress.

Meditation is an activity in which a person tries to shut off the outer world and tries to look inside himself to find answers. It is a process in which a person at least temporarily tries to gain control over his senses. During meditation, a person commands his senses to think what he wants to think rather than being commanded by his senses.

For me, it is a time when a person is directly in communication with me and receptive to my suggestions. Weather I am the inner voice or the Consciousness, meditation is the state in which a person is most likely to understand or hear me.

For most of his life, Shiv had a very limited ability to command any other bodily organ, and in turn, he had developed a mastery over the meditative state of mind. That's how he was in knowledge of many out of the world mysteries; including me.

I felt empowered when Shiv imagined and directed his Third Eye to see things as he wanted them to be. This is the way to establish direct communication with the universe and apprise the cosmos about the things you desire in your life. You can command the universe with your Third Eye.

As Shiv's concentration intensified, I felt a white glow illuminating the blank space around me. Slowly, the lighting intensified and then as if out of nowhere, a bluish glow appeared that slowly intensified and took a gaseous form. It was difficult to believe at first, but I was able to recognize the figure in a single instant.

CHAPTER 23

THE GRANTHI's

'Chit! Oh my God...Chit! My friend, where have you been? I missed you so much. I really needed you,' I was overjoyed at seeing Chit back.

'Well, I was always there with you, protecting you and guiding you in your pursuit of God,' Chit said.

'So much happened, you know. Marich attacked us and we barely survived, Sarvan and Vani broke up and Rohan and Vani patched up, and...and...' I was blabbering like a kid.

'I know...I know...I was also there throughout these happenings,' Chit said.

'You were? How? Where?' I asked, feeling surprised.

'I directed the hermit to tell you the story of Lord Ram's ring and now I am teaching you about Lord Krishna,' Chit said.

'You are Rohan's mother,' I almost yelled.

'No, I am the Consciousness that is guiding her and you,' Chit said.

It dawned upon me quickly. Chit was the Super consciousness that guided Lord Hanuman and is today a part of many humans; one of which was Rohan's mother. Chit was merely guiding Rohan's mother on the path of her Karma's. He was also my guru and forever guided me.

He was the force that was pushing me in pursuit of my destiny. He was the celestial power that was making coincidences happen in my life as I was enabling coincidences to happen in the lives of Mortal human bodies that I was controlling. It was all a game of Karma. There was a power behind every power that was guiding the path of every human wandering on the surface of Earth.

What humans called destiny was just interplay between these celestial supernatural forces that were directing controlled human bodies into different directions and in turn giving birth to an illusion called life to human beings.

'But then why did you let me face all the hardships? You know, Shiv and rest of the family members almost died?' I questioned.

'It was important to open your Granthis,' Chit said.

'What is that?' I asked.

'Granthi literally means knot. It is akin to keeping all the knowledge locked and protected so that only the truly worthy get access to it. So, if you are trying to find God, you need to prove your worthiness by passing three tests, one for each granthi.

Understanding God is a process in which you have to start understanding from infinity and arrive at unity or vice versa. You have already learnt about the seven chakras in the human body that can supply nature's energy directly to the human body. The magic happens when these chakras are connected by a channel that activates these chakras and directs them to the upward direction, towards God.

This happens with the rise of Kundalini. When it rises through the different chakras, it activates and connects the chakras, thus, flooding the human body with divine energy with which human beings can attain Siddhis to perform seemingly miraculous feats.

But this flow of Kundalini Shakti is restricted by three knots or granthi's that make the rise of Kundalini Shakti impossible till these granthi's are opened. Let me explain you what these granthi's are.

The three granthi's (psychic knots) in the physical body are obstacles on the path of the awakened Kundalini. The threegranthi's are called Brahma Granthi, Vishnu Granthi, and Rudra Granthi, and relate to the body, emotion, and mind respectively. Each aspirant must transcend these barriers to clear the way for the ascending Kundalini.

- **Brahma Granthi** - This granthi is situated at the Muladhara Chakra and also governs the Svadisthana Chakra. It implies attachment to physical pleasures, material objects, and excessive selfishness. It also implies overcoming Tamsik attributes like negativity, lethargy, and ignorance. It is also known as perineal knot. Once this blockage is removed from the realm of Consciousnessand energy, instincts of the deep rootedness and energy are released.
- **Vishnu Granthi**–This granthi is situated in the heart or Anahata Chakra, and also governs the Manipura Chakra. It is associated with the bondage of emotional attachment and attachment to people and inner psychic visions. It is connected to the Rajasik attributes like passion, ambition, and assertiveness. It is also known as the navel knot. Once the Vishnu Granthi blockage is removed, we begin to draw energy to sustain ourselves from the universe instead of the localized energy centres of the body like lungs or stomach.
- **Rudra Granthi**–This granthi is situated at the third eye or Ajna Chakra, and also governs the throat or Visuddha Chakra. It is associated with attachment to Siddhis, psychic phenomenon's, and understanding about one - self. One must surrender the sense of individual ego and transcend duality to make further spiritual progress. It is also known as forehead knot. Once Rudra Granthi blockage is removed, it leads to the evolution of a sixth sense or the eye of intuition, as the third eye of Lord Shiva. Ajna Chakra is where Ida and Pingla Nadi's merge and becomeone; hence, it is the place where duality becomes unity. It is where Shakti will meet Shiv and infinity will get dissolved into unity. After this, an individual is just one step away from finding God.

But it is not easy to open these granthi's. If a seeker truly wants to proceed on the path of attaining God, then he would have to prove his worthiness. Only the worthy can open these granthi's,' Chit said.

I pondered for a while over what chit had said and then asked, 'And how do you open these granthi's?'

'One can prove his worthiness by facing challenges and problems and still continuing on the path of God.

That is why I guided Rohan to find Shiv. So that all these humans could face the challenges that can prove their worthiness,' Chit said.

'You deliberately led them to all these troubles. Do you know they all could have died? Since the time Rohan has found Shiv, they have been through nothing but troubles,' I said angrily.

'Really? Do you think they were alive before that? All of them had reached a stalemate where their souls were rotting inside their bodies. They would have died anyway. Now they are going to live for a purpose; adivine purpose that will purify their souls and serve them in the after life. The fruits of their Karma's will stay with them in their subsequent births. There is a higher purpose associated with every human life and I have guided them on a path that can help them discover that,' Chit said.

'But how have all these troubles that we have faced helped us?' I inquired.

Chit appeared to have smiled at my question and said, 'You have yet not fully understood the plot.'

When Marich's men came to find you at Rohan's Goa house, the family members stood for you and you stood for the family members; you did that with absolute selflessness. It could have cost you your life but you gave up all attachments to the material world and stood for something you considered righteous. This selfless act freed you from the bondages of material world and opened your Brahma Granthi.

That was how Shiv was able to gain the power of emitting the vibrations of his choice that could evaporate bullets.

When Marich was killing the family members, you transcended

emotional bondages and found a way to leave your body and break through the barrier of time and space. This was an act by which you overcame all your fears and believed in your existence outside the human body. Your belief in Karma's beyond the web of time and space and even beyond this universe, opened your Vishnu Granthi.

That was how Shiv was able to gain access to divine powers and show that out - worldly form with his huge size and multiple arms. That is what happens when one attains Siddhi's. You get powers beyond the physical laws of this world.

Your progress in pursuit of God has been the result of your Karma's that you perform in different human bodies. There remains only one obstacle now. One final granthi–the Rudra Granthi,' Chit explained.

'Does that mean another war is coming my way?' I asked.

'To find God, first one has to win the war within,' Chit said.' the day you will realise who you are,you will also find God.' With these words, Chit disappeared.

Shiv opened his eyes to see Rohan's mother sitting opposite him. It seemed as if considerable time had lapsed since they sat meditating. He got up and touched her feet. As she kept her hand on hishead to bless him, he was filled with humility and warmth.

Shiv looked at Rohan's mother with tears in his eyes, 'I don't know if I will find God,' Shiv said,' but you, my guru, will remain greater than God to me.'

The moment was disturbed by Sarvan banging the door. Shiv opened the door to find Sarvan breathlessly panting.

'There is something happening in the sea. You need to see that,' Sarvan said.

PART III – GOD
(PURUSH+PRAKRITI)

CHAPTER 24

THE PANCH KOSHA

Shiv and Sarvan ran out of the house and were horror - struck when they looked towards the sea.

Somewhere half way down the extent of the ocean which could be witnessed by a naked human eye, stood a wall of water hundreds of feet high. The waves in this wall were rising upwards towards the sky. If the water descended, it could have engulfed the entirety of Goa, but the wall of water just stood there hanging by some mysterious force.

'There are weird stories all over the news.' the overwhelmed faces of Shiv and Sarvan were disturbed by the voice of Rohan's mother, 'I think you guys should come over here and watch the news.'

They both ran inside. All the news channels were reporting a strange phenomenon in Mumbai.

In an entirely bewildering act, the entire population of Mumbai was sitting in groups of thousands around local water bodiesin their areas and together they were chanting some kind of mantras.

The scene looked scary; their eyes were blank and the recital was in unison with each other. It was as if they were all participating in some kind of grand Yagna. Their strength was in millions. The recital of mantras grew louder till one could hear nothing other than the sound of the mantras.

A news reporter said, 'As bizarre as it may sound but the law and order machinery of the city of Mumbai has completely

In effect, one may say that Sharira or the human body is an outer covering for the Soul. But in fact, the human body itself is made up of five coverings. These are known as Pancha Kosha or five sheaths or five layers around the human soul.

- **Annamay Kosh (Food Sheath)**-Outermost of the Pancha koshas. The outermost of the koshas is called the sheath of food, or Annamaya Kosh. It is composed of Earth element.

It is the gross physical body. This is the sheath of the physical self, named from the fact that it is nourished by food. Annamay Kosh is' Matter' in the form of physical body sustained by the intake of food. It includes five actuatory organs or Karmindriyans. This sheath has the densest vibrational frequency and this kosha cannot exist without contact with the other koshas.

Personality of the individual i. e. physique as well as traits depend on the condition of Annamaya Kosh, the formation of which continues life after life. The physique in the next birth is decided by the state of Annamaya Kosh of earlier births. That is why old civilizations believed in preserving the physical bodies by mummification. Ancient Hindu wisdom also believes that man, his personality, and destiny (fate) are determined in his subtle bodies, which he brings from previous births.

When a person gets sick, modern medical science aims to treat this kosha, by balancing the chemical composition of hormones of the body.

But if this kosha is governed by Earth element and is just the conversion of food into body form, then there must be a life force governing it, an energy system to run the physical body; there comes the need for a second sheath to exist.

- **Pranmay Kosh (Vital Air Sheath)** - The second sheath is the Pranmay Kosh (the life force) and is governed by air element.

Pranmay Kosh is composed of Prana, the vital principle or the force that holds together the body and the mind. Its physical manifestation is the breath. As long as this vital principle exists in an organism, life continues. So basically, it is all the energy collapsed as the police and judiciary have themselves joined the event. It looks as if the people have either been possessed by some power or commanded by a supernatural power to do the same...with cameraman Praveen, this is Mandakini Sharma reporting from Bandra.'

'What are they doing? Is it some festival today?'Sarvan asked Shiv.

'I am not sure,' Shiv replied, attentively looking at the news broadcast.

'It looks like some kind of Yagna,' Rohan's mother said.

'What is a Yagna?' Shiv asked.

'Well, our scriptures mention that in earlier times, thousands of Brahmans used to sit around fire and recite mantras to please Gods. These mantras used to be so powerful that it used to force Gods to appear and grant wishes to the seekers.

These are stories for sure, but the concept is that you assemble the five elements together in the havan fire. These are Earth, water, fire, air, and space. After these elements are added to the havan agni, the saints collectively recite mantras which release a kind of vibration that can provide a Panch - Tatva (five element) or flesh and bone form to the energy form of God. Thus, these gods get manifested in the havan fire.

In modern times also, the practice continues but today no one remembers those powerful mantras. So, today it is generally being done for peace and well - being of the world,' Rohan's mother said.

'But how can an energy form of God be manifested into a flesh and bone human being just by adding all the five Tatvas?' Shiv asked.

'Let us finally understand human body,' Rohan's mother said.' the deep rooted concept behind all religions highlights the presence of a Soul or spirit inside a human body. It is finally this spirit that is the cause of all Karmas and after the death of the individual, it is this spirit that gets rewarded or punished for the Karmas performed by the human body.

that is required for the functioning of the Annamaya Kosh.

Yogic literature mentions the presence of 72,000 pathways along which the Prana moves in a human body. The pathways have been named as Nadis in Yoga. Nadis are astral tubes that carry Pranic currents. They cannot be seen with the naked eyes. They are not the ordinary nerves, arteries, and veins. These 72,000 nadis interconnect the energetic centres or chakras in a human body.

Even though the form of this sheath is subtle, it is very similar to the form of the physical body. All medical science that aims to regulate the energy flow in human body like acupuncture, reiki, magneto - therapy, Kundalini etcwork on this kosha. Homeopathic medicines in moderate potencies also act on this kosha.

But with only a body and a life force, human body would be something akin to the modern day machines with mechanical parts forming the body and electricity being provided by the Prana. But to run every machine there has to be a man, because a machine cannot think and decide.

So, there is someone behind this powered machine of the human body that can feel and perceive and decide between good and bad. There is something that gets affected by all the sensory inputs experienced by the human body. If ten people see the same scene, then all ten of them will be affected by the scene differently. The same scene will invoke different feelings in different human beingsand therein comes the third sheath.

- <u>Manomay Kosh (Mind Sheath)-</u>Manomaya means composed of manas or mind. It governs actions like feelings, emotions, and memories. The mind along with the five sensory organs is said to constitute the Manomaya Kosh or the mind - sheath.

The Manomaya Kosh is the mental faculty that receives all the sensory inputs from brain and interprets them as good or bad.

When your eyes see the colour red,they cannot interpret what colour they have seen and send the data to your brain. It is your brain which finally confers that the colour seen by your eyes was red. But there is something else which decides whether red is a good or bad colour. This something is mind. So, mind can categorise the output produced by the brain as good or bad.

Hence, mind is the cause of personal likes and dislikes. Man's bondage is caused by the mind, and liberation too, is caused by mind alone.

This kosha is much more powerful than the preceding two koshas and governs them and is, in turn, governed by the two koshas superior to it.

It is, thus, central to human existence. Many treatment therapies like aroma, music, colour, placebo therapy, and shamanism work upon this kosha.

So, now we have a body, a life force that provides all the energy that the body needs to provide the multifarious tasks, and a mind which can interpret the inputs of the sensory organs as good or bad. But human behaviour depicts something strange.

Despite the mind telling them something is bad, they can wilfully ignore their mind and choose to do it. If a person has diabetes and the intake of sweet can harm him, the mind will come to the obvious conclusion that sweet is bad but the mind still cannot refrain a person from having something sweet.

This something is different from mind as it does not take inputs from the sensory organs. In fact, it does not take inputs from any physical organ at all. It does the thinking part purely based on its memory or experiences or desires. So, even mind is inferior to the kosha superior to it.

Thus, there exists another kosha that is governing the actions of the outer three koshas. This kosha which governs mind is called Vigyanmay Kosha or the sheath of intellect.

- **Vigyanmay Kosh (Intellect Sheath)** - The Sharira, Prana, and Mind constitute a perfectly functional entity called a human being but such a human being will only be governed by the primal instincts.

All animals have these first three sheaths. What differentiates human beings from rest of the animals is the presence of a fourth sheath called the Vigyanmaya Kosh that provides them with a feeling of individuality or ego.

The feeling of me and mine, the capability of intelligent discrimination, will, and reasoning constitutes Vigyanmaya Kosh. It provides the capability of unique thinking to every single human being.

When one closes their eyes and relaxes during meditation, the functioning of the Manomaya Kosh becomes minimal. The Vigyanmaya Kosh comes in the front and gets active. In the final stages of meditation, the intellect becomes stable and mind becomes still, and this is called Samadhi.

Meditation when used as a therapeutic tool works in the Vigyanmaya Kosh. All sorts of reasoning and counselling (psychiatric - therapy) also act on this kosha.

But, even this knowledge sheath cannot be the supreme self for the reason that it is subject to change, it is temporary and limited, and it will perish with the human body.

So, there has to be something that is even inside his body that is permanent and will outlive the human body. That is the doer of all the Karma's and will be subjected to the results mentioned by religions after the death of the outer body.

- **Aanandmay Kosh (Bliss Sheath)–Innermost of the Pancha koshas.** The fifth sheath or the Anandmaya Kosh is the innermost kosha in close proximity to the Soul.

The bliss sheath normally has its fullest play during deep sleep; while in the dreaming and wakeful states, it has only a partial manifestation.

This kosha is a reflection of the three divine qualities of the Soul, namely Sat, Chit, and Anand. Sat means that it is true and eternal. Chit means that it is alive and conscious (the characteristic that separates the living and the non - living). And Anand means that it is full of bliss in itself.

Being joyful is a prominent characteristic of this kosha. Since the Soul itself is a non - doer of anything, its qualities are manifested through this innermost kosha. This is realised when we reach Samadhi.'

Rohan's mother became very quiet as soon as she completed the narration of the five sheaths.

'I have understood,' Shiv said.' so under these five sheaths resides the Atman or the Soul?'

Rohan's mother pondered for a while and said,' No, that is not what my grandma said. My grandma told me that there is nothing under it.'

'What!' Shiv said,' what do you mean? There must be a Soul inside these five sheaths; that Soul which is Me.'

'It should be, but my grandma said there is nothing under the fifth kosha…it's just vacant,' Rohan's mother again said.

'But then…then…Who am I?' Shiv asked.

Deep inside I had been longing to ask the same question.

'You will have to discover it yourself,' Rohan's mother said. 'I have just told you all that I learnt from my grandmother but there is one last thing that I can do to help you out.'

'What's that?' Shiv asked.

'There is one last story I can tell you that might help you in your pursuit of God,' Rohan's mother said and narrated the last story to Shiv.

When the story ended, Shiv just stared in bewilderment at Rohan's mother face.

'Shiv, you need to see this.' Sarvan's words drew everyone's attention towards the television set.

The moment Shiv saw the news, he was flabbergasted.

At the top floor office of Tripura Pharmaceuticals Pvt Ltd. Rohan, Vani, and Santy watched helplessly the giant screens that were now showing news broadcast from all over the countryside.

After the first missile strike at Mumbai, similar strikes were conducted at the coastal areas of Cochin, Kolkata, Kerala, and Visakhapatnam. The results were strikingly similar at all the places. People with blank eyes just gathered around a waterbody and recited mantras.

It took the trio some time to assimilate what Marich was upto. The next scene that flashed on the screen made his intentions clear and scared the air out of the lungs of the three of them.

The Ellora Caves in Aurangabad district of Maharashtra, India are rock - cut cave monuments which date from the 2nd century BCE to about 480 or 650 CE. The majestic design of these caves stands testimony to the fact that there existed a very scientifically advanced society prior to the arrival of human beings. A careful study of these architectural marvels stands next only to the great Pyramids in evoking mysticism.

There are over 100 caves at the site; all excavated from the basalt cliffs in the Charanandri Hills, 34 of which are open to public. They were created mainly between the fifth and tenth centuries by Buddhist, Hindu, and Jain monks.

Oddly, they were carved from top to bottom. The priests hollowed out the ceiling first, and worked down, placing pillars as they went. An entire mountain, cut by hand into places of worship, held from collapse by elaborately carved columns and decorated with colossal statues from the three major religions.

Among the most visibly awe inspiring structures at the Ellora site is Temple Kailasa dedicated to Lord Shiva, less romantically known as Cave 16.

Kailasa temple is an engineering marvel. It is a three - storeyed temple adorned with spectacular carvings cut from a single rock within the face of a mountain, with zero margins for error.

Outer walls open into an airy courtyard, surrounded on three sides by columned chambers set deep into the cliff. In the centre is a free - standing, delicately carved temple, smothered in sculptures depicting scenes from the Ramayana and flanked by rows of life - size elephants, most of whose trunks have succumbed to centuries of vandalism.

The sheer amount of the effort required to erect such a structure is staggering. Archaeologists consider that this mammoth temple would have been built in approximately 18 years after digging out around 4,00,000 tons of rock. If we calculate roughly, it would amount to 60 tons of rock daily and that too with the hammer, chisel, and picks.

18 years of error - free hard work by hundreds of skilled craftsmen, who then, for some reason just left it and disappeared. This is the single largest monolithic structure on Earth. It is the epitome of a millennium of rock - cut architecture in India that was never again surpassed, or even attempted.

However, the most well - preserved secret about Ellora caves is not what is seen above the Earth; it is what lies beneath.

Ellora caves have convincing evidence about a secret underground area that is hidden under these caves. There is a tunnel over 40 feet deep and then it takes a right angle turn to proceed underground. Nobody knows what's inside becauseafter that, the tunnel becomes too narrow for human beings to get through it. In fact, the entire area is infused with numerous small rectangular passages that go straight underground into unexplored depths.

Where do these mysterious tunnels lead? Who could have used such narrow passages? How can you carve such narrow passages if human beings cannot even get through them? Was it carved by humans at all? These are questions unanswered till now.

The Kailasha Temple in Ellora Caves was in news today because ever since the recital of mantra's had started, there have been hundreds of snakes that were emerging out from the fissures beneath the rocky structure. At first the size of the snakes was small, but as time passed they grew larger and larger.

At around half past ten, huge tentacles came out from beneath the temple. These tentacles were enormous and extended uptill the height of the temple. Similar tentacles started emerging out from other caves as well. As the tentacles emerged, they uprooted the trees and broke through the hill side.

At the sea front all around the Indian peninsula,a huge wall of water had erected similar to the one at Goa. It was as if the entire of India had been cut off from the rest of the world by that wall of sea water.

At last, around midday,they emerged from beneath the ground.

CHAPTER 25

THE RISE OF THE ASURAS

Rohan, Vani, and Santy looked at the giant screen with horror as images of strange ghastly creatures emerging from the ground from below the surface of the Earth started flashing.

These creatures were almost twenty feet in size and had a half human and half serpentine shape, with their human part extending waist upwards. They had brownish black skin tone and a slimy tail under their muscular torso. They had dual cavities instead of nose as if their nose had been cut, and they had long flowing hair. They had long fangs and pointed teeth giving them a draconian look and they spoke with a hissing sound. And from head to tail, they were adorned with gold ornaments.

The most striking feature was their eyes. Their eyes were completely white. They had no pupils. They were blind.

They appeared in hundreds, and it was destruction right from the moment they appeared. It took a few hours for them to silence the pandemonium that ensued amongst the tourists that were present on the site at that moment. They were simply too gigantic, too ferocious, and too hungry for the unsuspecting tourists. The Ellora site was soon splattered in blood and human flesh. As they ate their fill, they all started slithering in the same direction,in the direction of Mumbai.

There was a faint smile on Marich's face as he spoke.

'Tell the pilots to start the helicopter. The time has come for the King to arrive. I will go myself to greet him in Goa. And take these three into the temple,' Marich said, pointing towards the trio.

At the coast of Goa, hundreds had gathered to watch the natural phenomenon that was unfolding in form of the giant wall of water that had erected.

The native people of Goa had forever depended upon the sea for everything they had. For these native Goans, who had spent their lives watching the sea, it was the most spectacular moment they were witnessing and they stood there spellbound.

And the moment indeed turned more spectacular when the water walls started to convex till a huge flying object appeared from underneath the water wall.

The flying object was enormous in its dimensions and covered an area of hundreds of square feet underneath. The base of the flying object was circular in shape and it tapered towards the top. Close to the top, there were four exhausts facing the top. Between the four exhausts was a giant transparent cone right at the top.

The entire flying thing appeared like a giant flying mountain of gold. Yes, it was all golden in colour.

'It's...it's Rukma Vimana!'someone exclaimed from the crowd. 'I have seen the images of these ancient flying machines on the internet.'

Soon, more and more vimanas began to appear from behind the wall of water. They were all of different types and sizes. The vimana's emerged out of the wall and just came to hover about fifty meters above the coast.

Vimanas started dissipating in different directions. The biggest golden vimana just stood there in mid - air. Then, as Shiv and Sarvan looked on, four doors opened on the lower portion of the vimana and more figures of serpentine men started appearing out.

Finally, the largest half - serpent half - man appeared. He was almost twice the size of the other serpentine demons and infinite times more frightening. He looked and behaved like the King of the demons that were unleashed on Earth.

The serpentine men were dressed in gold and armed with some kind of bows and arrows. The creatures were savages. They had come from hell, and the moment they touched the surface of Earth, hell is what they unleashed on Earth.

Humans were just no match for the might of those giants. They tossed human bodies and split them open with their sharp nails. They massacred every living thing in sight and more than that, they seemed to be developing a liking for it.

Within a few minutes, the seashore of Goa was covered in human blood and flesh. The onlookers who were anticipating the appearance of divine Gods from these un Earthly vimana's were not given much time for regretting it.

Shiv and Sarvan ran for cover into Rohan's house as a number of serpents leapt towards them. Rohan's mother was missing from the house. They were able to temporarily confuse the serpentine men in the maze of Rohan's ancestral house and buy just enough time to make a decision.

'We need to run into the sea,' Shiv said,' that's the only place which will give us shelter even for a few moments.' While the serpentine men searched for them inside the house, Shiv and Sarvan ran towards the sea and submerged themselves completely.

Below the mayhem on the surface, the sea was still protecting and nourishing the life under it. For a moment, Sarvan felt as if he had come home. The colourful corals illuminated a complete world hidden from the human world. The vivid society of sea creatures of infinite different forms had manifested into a profound ecosystem that existed in perfect harmony in the sea. These sea creatures were born out of the sea and later, they dissolved within it. There must be a God of these creatures also.

Shiv momentarily took his head out of the water to refill his breath only to notice that Sarvan had not emerged out for some time now. He again dived in to find Sarvan.

Shiv found Sarvan sitting on the ocean floor in a poised Dhyan

Mudra with a gentle smile on his lips. He was neither moving nor breathing and yet, he appeared to be completely alive to everything around him.

'It is impossible,' Shiv thought to himself,' no one can hold his breath that long. I will have to get him out else he will die.'

Shiv swam close to Sarvan and tried to touch Sarvan's rock still body.

In Sarvan's head, I felt my grip loosening on his brain. I was not receiving any input from any of his Indriyans. No dreams were flashing inside his mind. It had never happened to me before. I had witnessed death before, but this was something different from death. Unlike death, there was no fear in Sarvan's mind; on the contrary, he was blissfully contented.

It felt as if the flow of emotions had completely stopped in his mind. It felt as if the cluster of thousands of different kinds of vibrations which form the human body had somehow synchronised inside Sarvan's mind. All the vibrations which form thoughts, emotions, dreams, and memories had all streamlined into a single wavelength of frequency. A single beat.

Suddenly, there was a bright flash of white light.

The next moment, I found myself looking at Sarvan through Shiv's eyes. Some mysterious light had forced me out of Sarvan's brain. At first, it was hard for me to believe that I can be forced out of a human body that I commanded against my will.

Shiv was trying to move Sarvan's body but all his efforts were failing. Sarvan's body was still like a stone boulder and the smile on his face glittered like corals on the face of stones.

'Leave it. Let him be there,' I told Shiv.

'Is he dead?' Shiv asked.

'He is neither living nor dead,' I said,' maybe this is the state that they call Samadhi.'

CHAPTER 26

THE POWER OF SOUND

Rohan, Vani, and Santy had been shifted inside a huge hall surrounded by tall pillars all around. The engravings on the walls and pillars implied that the hall was the inside of some giant ancient temple.

At a raised platform in the front, Marich stood naked and drenched in blood with Aghora to his side; a giant serpentine man was standing in front of him holding Marich by his shoulders and looking directly into his eyes. After a few minutes of interaction, the serpentine man hissed out a deep breath that covered Marich's face like a cloud of smoke.

Marich dropped unconscious to the ground. The serpentine man slithered inside a dark fissure in a corner of the temple.

'You bastards! What have you brought upon Earth?' Rohan yelled at Aghora.

Aghora turned towards Rohan. 'I deliberately kept you guys alive; someone must be there to appreciate the success of our grand plan,' Aghora said.

'You have unleashed an army of demons to massacre the human race out of existence,' Rohan said, in an angry tone with tears in his eyes.

'No…I don't want to massacre the human race into extinction. I just want to scare them into submission. Why don't you guys understand, human beings are worthless and unguided without Gods to rule over them. That is exactly what I am providing them. You see this bloodshed is just the initial part to gain unquestioned submission from the human race.

Once humans accept the Nag Vansh as their true rulers and Takshak as their ultimate king, it all stops and humans can then happily serve their kings forever.

Isn't it all that humans have ever wanted–to obediently serve their Gods? Well, here they are. The superior race of Gods is there for you to worship. As soon as they establish their supremacy, humans can start worshipping them,' Aghora said.

'You will never win this fight against us,' Rohan said.

Aghora laughed at Rohan.' You surprise me by your stupidity. Who said we are here to fight you? We are here to fight against the Devas. You humans are the element who will assist us in that fight.

Why do you think we Asuras remained confined to the lower worlds for so long? And why do you think we have appeared now?

We are here due to human effort only. Did you witness all that chanting by millions of people together? I don't think it would have been possible without that.

Humans have called the Asura race from Nag - Loka to rule over them. Of course, I and Marich had to work for years to make that possible, to slowly destroy the pineal gland in human bodies, to discover the chemicals and vibrations that can control human brains, and finally,to conduct the world's greatest Yagna to empower the Nags to surface on Earth. It has been a very long journey.' Aghora was lost in transition for a moment.

'But what kind of help you aim to get by controlling the human race?' Vani asked, grabbing Aghora's attention.

Aghora turned towards Vani and spoke again,' You humans don't know the power of sound; you used to know but as the yuga changed, you have forgotten. So before I own you completely, let me remind you. The process of creation involves creating something out of nothing, and the process of destruction involves dissolving something into nothing.

When a star or a galaxy dies, it collapses into itself until nothing remains. Even today, most of the volume of the universe is nothing. This nothingness comprises 95% of the universe. Scientists today have started using the word dark matter to describe this nothingness.

To create anything you need energy, and the most primary form of energy is light. As it is written in the Bible that out of nothing God created light. So, if you have to create energy out of nothing, it can be done in the form of light.

But light energy moves in a straight line. Without an external force, it cannot bend. Neither can it give shape to anything nor can its frequency and wavelength be changed. So, it is pertinent that we have another superior form of energy that can bend light energy and give shape to it so that it can be moulded into matter.

That other superior form of energy is sound. Even the Bible says that first, God said "let there be light", and then there was light. That means sound existed before even light. So, sound is what created energy or light.

The study of cymantics is a science which deals with everything in the world that is influenced by Sound waves. We can produce fantastic shapes in powdered solid or water or even fire just by passing sound waves through it. So, sound is the energy which makes creation a possibility. Sound is the first step from non - creation into creation.

Now consider this; inside an ocean, a water droplet has no existence despite the fact that the ocean is made up of water droplets. But if we pass sound through ocean, it will give rise to waves. Thus, into the nothingness of an ocean,wavy shapes have been created. If we keep increasing the intensity of sound, the shapes will get more profound.

But, by manifesting a wave from an un - manifested ocean, we have limited the infinite ocean form into a limited waveform, which is going to vanish into the ocean the moment sound is removed.

So, creation is nothing but limiting the form of the infinite with the help of sound.

Creation means a limited form; it may be a human being, a planet, or even a galaxy, but still, it is a limited form because whatever maybe the size of the wave it is limited as compared to the ocean.

Destruction means dissolving the manifested or finite into the infinite. If you destroy a solid, it loses its form but it also gets converted into its original and infinite energy form. That is why Lord Shiva is considered the greatest God because when he destroys, he removes the illusion and returns everything back to its original infinite form.

Lord Brahma, the creator, in his process of creation has limited the form of the infinite into numerous limited forms that give them the notion of creation and Lord Shiv, the destroyer, removes this illusion by returning everything back into its infinite form.

The infinite substance within and from which finite and limited forms are being created and destroyed is Lord Vishnu. You can understand Vishnu like an infinite ocean on which waves are created by passing sound as I explained in the above example.

For how long the creation is going to exist depends upon the duration for which sound is going to prevail, keeping the waves of the ocean in existence. In Hinduism, 'Om' is considered this sound of creation.

There are frequencies of sound which provide vibrational connection of all things living or non - living; these are known as natural frequencies.

432Hz is known as the healing tone and is associated with nature's ability to heal itself. It produces healing vibrations for mind, body, and spirit. Greatest musicians like Mozart and Beethoven used this 432Hz to tune their music. It is also used in healing medical science. Great ancient civilizations like India and Egypt also had their music instruments tuned to this frequency. Playing and listening to music that has been tuned to 432Hz would make your body and the organic world which surrounds it resonate in a natural way. 432Hz music resonates inside your body, releases emotional blockages, and expands Consciousness. Such music allows you to tune into the knowledge of the universe around us in a more intuitive way.

However, today the worldwide standard has been chosen as 440Hz instead of 432Hz. This happened when some authorities found out the negative effects that musical frequencies have on human behaviour and used it to gain control of the human race.

440Hz, despite being forced upon us as a music pitch tuning standard, is not in harmony with the frequency of Earth. We are part of Mother Nature, and therefore, playing the music that isn't tuned at the brain frequency over a prolonged period of time will make you feel out of sync. 440Hz is an unnatural tone which is not found anywhere in nature. Listening to music tuned to the disharmonic 440Hz frequency does harm you by causing stress, negative behaviour, and unstable emotions. The effect of it can be predominantly seen upon the human race today.

Humankind has been an unsuspecting victim of a frequency war on human consciousness that has been waged for decades. The goal has been to keep themas subservient as possible. People listening to this music are essentially prisoners of their own aggressive Consciousness.

If people can understand the dynamics of energy, frequency, and sound, they will be able to unlock unlimited potentials. There are also other frequencies that are natural frequencies in tune with nature.

Other common natural frequencies that are known to affect human bodies are:

- 396 Hz - This tone turns sadness into happiness by liberating a man from fear.
- 417 Hz - This tone removes mental trauma and facilitates easy recovery from bad memories.

- 528 Hz - This is known as the miracle tone and is often associated with DNA repair. It resonates with the human body and nature.
- 638 Hz - This tone strengthens tolerance and love and builds up relationships.
- 741 Hz - This tone increases self - confidence and improves expressive abilities.
- 852 Hz - This tone helps improve intuitive abilities and enables spiritual progress.
- 963 Hz - This tone purifies the spirit and resets it to its original self.

Well, of course, I and Marich discovered many more frequencies by which we are today controlling the behaviour of the human race. We did it by discovering the ability of sound to manipulate water.

Do you guys know that modern scientists have discovered that water has memory?' Aghora said.

CHAPTER 27

WATER HAS MEMORY

'Water has memory! How is that possible? Isn't it a non - living entity?' Santy spoke in a bewildered tone.

'Yes! Your human scientists have only discovered it, or maybe, re - discovered it,' Aghora said.' Water is the only substance that naturally exists in all the three states; solid, liquid, and gaseous. It has the highest surface tension of all liquids. It is the most powerful solvent on Earth. It defies gravity when it climbs the gigantic fissures inside the Earth's crust against tons of atmospheric pressure.

Water has a fixed chemical composition, but its molecular structure keeps changing. Its molecules get organised around each other to form molecular clusters. These clusters work like some type of memory cells. In fact, its molecular cluster takes its shape according to the external influences it faces.

So, you can say that the Molecular Structure of water is like an alphabet and the Molecular Cluster is like a sentence.

Water makes an imprint of any outside influence, remembering everything that occurred in the environment it has passed through.

If we photograph a droplet of water that has flown through its natural course along a river, it will show beautifully formed gentle clusters, whereas if we photograph a droplet of tap water which has been forced through pipes with bends at right angles it will show distorted and uneven clusters. In short, water with bad memory becomes contaminated and is likely to have a negative effect on the human body.

That's the reason many ancient civilisations chose to store water in brass or Earthen pots for some time before consuming it so that its molecular cluster returns to normal. A silver vessel can turn ordinary water into healing water by reorganising the molecular cluster of the water kept in it. In an experiment, a scientist had discovered that if the natural frequencies mentioned earlier or the music of great musicians is played near water, the water molecules get arranged into beautiful geometrical shapes.

If music can have that effect on water, imagine what effect it can have on human bodies which are 72% water. You can do anything by exposing humans to a particular type of sound,' Aghora said.

'I understand how you are controlling the human race,' Rohan said.' What I fail to understand is why you are doing this, considering you and Marich also won't survive this monster race after they finish all of us.'

'We are the last descendants of the remaining Asuras that were left after the war of Mahabharata that ended the rule of Devas and Asurason Earth and we have been chosen to rule the human race by the Nag king, Takshak, once they win over the Devas and their six worlds,' Aghora said.

'And you think you can keep the human race enslaved forever?' Vani asked.

'Of course, after the powers that Takshak has granted Marich, we definitely will,' Aghora said.

At the background of Aghora, a giant figure was rising. Marich had gained Consciousness.

CHAPTER 28

HEART VS BRAIN

When Shiv raised his head above the water surface, his face bore the expressions of a heartbroken man. Over time, he had developed a deep liking for the carefree and brooding nature of Sarvan; in fact, he used to feel a deeper spiritual connection.

Shiv had watched Sarvan's body motionless and devoid of any heartbeat sitting on the ocean floor with a secret smile still playing on his lips that had characterised Sarvan ever since he time travelled.

Without Sarvan and with the enormous fleet of demons standing in front of him, for the first time, Shiv felt lonely.

There is a limit till which a human being can be subdued using the fear factor, but the minute he loses all options to run away from fear, he gains the ability to face his fears.

Shiv swam back towards the beach and then emerged out of the sea till he was submerged waist - deep in water. He approached the giant serpentine man who was still standing just a little away from the shore and challenged the one who appeared to be the king of those demonsat the top of his voice.

'You have made a mistake coming out of your snake holes. It would have been best if you had remained hidden under the Earth,' Shiv said while tying the Shree - Yantra given by Rohan's mother on his forehead.

The loud cry made the huge muscular bust turn from its snake waist to face Shiv.

The king of demons appeared like a towering mountain in front of the petite frame of Shiv. There was a cloud of venomous smoke that came out of his open nostrils with every breath. His eyes glittered like ambers and he made a hissing sound with every sentence as his words echoed through the sky.

'It'ssss indeed surprising to see a mortal man challenging Takshaksss; the king of Nagssss, I can melt humanssss with just one looksss; you have to be someone specialsss to have the courage to stand in front of meeee. We have arrived to reclaim our kingdom and no onesss shall be able to stopsss it nowsss,' takshak said.

Shiv closed his eyes and gathered all the power that he had gained till now.

I amassed all the knowledge that I had earned and used it to channelize energy through all the 72000 nadis in Shiv's body. The five lower chakras opened up like engines flooding Shiv's nadis with enormous amounts of cosmic energy. As the energy forced the Kundalini Shakti through the fifth chakra, Shiv began to grow in size. Shiv grew into a muscular giant till he stood equal in size in front of Takshak.

'I recognizesss youss nowsss, it is indeed strangesss; so many yearsss and you are still heresss to meet meeesss. Glad to meet yousss; my old enemyssss,' takshak said, looking deep into Shiv's eyes.

'Old enemy?' Shiv asked.' I have never known any of your kind ever.'

'I am not talkingsss to yoursss mortal bodysss,' takshak said. 'I am speakingsss to the one who is inside yousss.'

I was stunned to hear the last words of Takshak. I took a deeper look at Takshak's face. I felt as if his amber eyes were looking through Shiv's body directly towards me. Takshak had completely ignored Shiv's bodily appearance and acknowledged my existence as the driver of all the bodily powers that Shiv was depicting.

It was the strangest thing I had encountered amidst everything that I had encountered, but what was even more outlandish was the fact that Takshak spoke of an older connection between me and him, and the fact that Takshak knew more about my past than I had discovered. Was it possible that like Chit, Naina, and Rohan's mother's Consciousness, even I had a past?

'Yousss becomes moress and moresss pathetic everytime that we meetsss; I wouldsss likesss to destroy you this timesss,' takshak said and flexed his muscles and drew a sword out of its sheath. As Takshak swung the sword, a lightning ray hit Shiv on the chest and he was thrown behind.

Shiv got up and released a wave of vibrations that made Takshak slither and duck down. The exchange of blows between Shiv and Takshak grew intense with every passing moment.

Despite my empowerment due to the spiritual growth I had experienced, the human body of Shiv was no match to the divine frame of Takshak. With every blow, Takshak drained out a portion of Shiv's energy that depleted his strength.

Takshak hissed out a large cloud that engulfed Shiv into its toxicity and made him fall on his knees. With Shiv pinned to the ground, Takshak rained lightning blows one after another on him.

Shiv was exhausted and profusely bleeding. A stream of blood was draining out of his forehead into the sea.

Takshak strangled Shiv into his tail and lifted him up. The grip tightened forcing air out of Shiv's lungs and immobilising him in front of Takshak. Takshak raised his sword for a final blow that would separate Shiv's head from his body.

I was watching helplessly as Takshak drew his sword back and opened his mouth in anticipation, showing his deadly fangs.

Suddenly, inside the closed darkchamber of Shiv's brain, there was an illumination. A bright white light engulfed the darkness and filled his brain with energy. Shiv's nadis flexed with a splurge of energy as the five chakras infused a renewed flux of divine cosmic energy into them.

A jet of water exploded between Shiv and Takshak, engulfing both of them completely and dragging them into the depth of the ocean. But to my surprise, the water did not drown Shiv. He found no difficulty in breathing. In fact, I felt energised by the sea.

'No one messes around with my friend.' Even in the turmoil of war, I was unmistaken in recognising the voice of Sarvan. I looked around but Sarvan was nowhere around, and yet the voice kept sounding,' You may be a race of Gods superior to the Mortal human race but you forgot that the human race is not protected by humans alone; it is also protected by nature.' Sarvan's voice was coming from all around. It was coming from the water.

Rohan, Vani, and Santy watched as Marich stood up in his giant naked frame in front of them. His body was glistening with blood. He had grown two horns on his head and looked draconian with long pointed nails and ripping muscles. His last encounter with the serpentine people had depleted him of whatever remains of humanity he had left in him.

'You guys have irritated me enough, but now with the blessing of Guru Shukaracharya, I can clearly recognise each one of you,' Marich said and turned towards Vani.

'I can see you hiding behind the face of this girl called Naina,' Marich said looking towards Vani. 'It's time to end what we started many years back.'

Marich broke the shackles that were restraining Vani and lifted her in the air by her neck.

'I wish you had supported me, Naina,' Marich said, holding Vani close to his face.' We could have made this happen much before.' Marich's grip tightened around Vani's neck.

Rohan had managed to free his legs from the rope and with his hand tied behind his back, he ran into Marich and pushed him backwards. Marich threw Vani to one side.' How many times do I have to end your pathetic existence?' Marich said to Rohan and threw him into a temple pillar.

While Marich was throwing Rohan around, Santy freed himself from the ropes and leapt towards the side bag hung from the shoulder of an unsuspecting Aghora.

Aghora's bag was full of numerous kinds of powders. Santy opened a small box and threw it to the ground. The powder erupted on striking the ground into a cloud of smoke that temporarily blinded everyone.

By the time the smoke cleared, Rohan had picked up a Trishul lying next to the idol of Lord Shiva and struck Marich with that. The Trishul pierced into Marich's right thigh and made him cry in pain.

Marich was furious and threw a large temple boulder towards Rohan. Rohan barely escaped the boulder, thankfully due to his athletic build.

As Santy was trying to find more chemicals from Aghora's bag, Marich leapt and held his hand. Then Marich lifted Santy in the air with both his hands and in one move,brought him down and smashed his back against his knee. Marich then threw the motionless body of Santy to one side.

'Nooooo,' Rohan cried and ran towards Marich with an iron rod in his hand, but before he could reach Marich, he was hit by a ball of fire. Aghora had by now taken control of his bag and was using his power of alchemy to fight against Rohan and Vani.

As Rohan dropped to the ground, partly burned by the ball of fire, Marich picked him up.

Before Marich could use his grip to rip apart Rohan into two pieces, Vani emerged out from behind a temple pillar and stood in front of Marich.

'Leave him, it is me that you want,' Vani said.

Marich stopped for a moment and said, 'I don't want either of you. It is death that I want for both of you.' then Marich lifted both Rohan and Vani with one hand each.

I felt divided. While on one side I was fighting Takshak as a part of Shiv, on the other hand, I was fighting Marich as part of

Rohan. Two different bodies fighting different battles against different enemies with the same central Consciousness that was me.'

While Shiv had some advantage of an energised Kundalini that empowered him with Siddhis, Rohan had nothing; or so I thought.

Rohan had another advantage that I was soon to discover.

I discovered that because for the first time, I felt a new beat reverberating faintly amidst all the chaos.

The original sound beat that was the cause of all creation.

This beat made me realize that my understanding of the human body was only half complete. There was another half that I was yet to understand.

It was because till now, I had only restricted myself to the understanding of the human brain. I believed that the brain alone controls the entire functioning of the human body. I was wrong because, despite its unquestioned importance, the brain is still not considered as a symbol of life by mankind.

In all my understanding till now I had considered my control over the human brain as the source of all the powers that a human being can portray. But in this heat of the moment, I realized my mistake;the fact that I was not exercising even half of my potential over the human body.

Since time immortal, all the civilizations of the world have given importance to another body organ as the Seat of Life and Consciousness above the human brain; and all the religious scriptures perfectly subscribe to this belief by referring that human organ as the symbol of life over any other human organ. That organ is the Human Heart.

Since ancient times, the heart has been considered the source of emotions, courage, and wisdom. Mankind has used popular slangs like 'mighty heart' to portray courage, 'cold heart' to portray lack of emotions, 'pure heart' to describe nobility, and 'heartbroken' to portray sadness.

All the religious scriptures commonly agree when they say 'let your heart guide you' as they believe only the heart can guide a human being on the true path of God.

In Christianity, Jesus Christ is depicted with a heart, in ancient Egypt, people worshipped the heart as the true source of all knowledge and in Hinduism, every single form of God is known to form a hearty alliance with their escorts and their followers.

Even the two most beautiful creations of God have been demarcated clearly by these two bodily organs. Men think from their brainswhile women think from their heartsand that is the basic difference between the functioning of these two pillars of human existence.

If feelings and emotions are real and powerful sources of energy that manifest in the true form and create the reality that every human being lives in, then what about the organ that has been connected with all these most powerful emotions known to mankind.

Happiness and sadness have been associated with the heart. Friendship and animosity are the relations established by one's heart. Greed and patience have also been associated with the heart. Instincts have been associated with the heart. Courage and cowardice have been associated with heart and even the most powerful emotion called love has been solely associated with the heart.

What does this mean? Why has it been advocated to mankind that in the most difficult times, they should allow themselves to be guided by their hearts? Can the human heart think? Can it guide the human brain? What exactly is this best kept open secret about the human heart?

After all, if we believe heart to be just a pump for supplying blood to the human body, then it would be plain stupid to associate it with any kind of feeling or emotion. And yet mankind has since forever differentiated between matters of mind and matters of the heart and given priority to matters ofheart over matters of the mind.

In modern science, when the surgeons perform operations of

different human organs their experiences are surreal, when they cut open a human body, all individual organs appear lifeless except one. The liver looks like a dead piece of flesh, the stomach like a cavity, and even the brain just sits there with no visible activity at all, but when they open a heart, it seems to be a completely different living entity hidden beneath the protection of one's chest jumping with life. It seems to be dancing to a tune of its own–a poetry of life. Let me explain this mystery and unravel the secret.

The heart is the first organ to function during the foetus development process. The first heartbeats are considered as an inveterate sign of life in a foetus.

In fact, the heart starts to function within 20 days after conception whereas the brain does not function until after roughly 90 days. So, when life starts in a baby, it starts without a brain with only the heart controlling all early part of development. A mother's brainwaves can synchronize to her baby's heartbeats creating the first bond between them. Also, the heart is a powerful electromagnetic field generator that acts asa broadcasting device. As the heart beats, it sends out electromagnetic waves that contain essential information. These waves of information are received by all cells of the foetus. Therefore, they affect how the foetus is developed.

The brain and the heart are both electromagnetic field generators but as an established fact, the heart is up to hundred times electrically stronger and up to five to six thousand times magnetically stronger as compared to a brain. The magnetic field of the human heart can be experienced several feet away from their bodies and we have already established the fact that the spectrum of electromagnetic field comprises the entire range of frequencies that constitute the physical world that we live in.

The electromagnetic field generated by the heart changes in accordance with our emotions. Positive emotions improve immunity whereas negative emotions have a damaging effect on the body.

With the help of modern pieces of equipment, it has been established that the heart does not beat at a regular rate as was initially assumed. In fact, even a healthy heart beats at an irregular rate.

The emotions we experience, directly affect our heart rhythmic pattern. In a state of anger, anxiety, and depression, the heart rhythm pattern is irregular and disturbed whereas, in a state of happiness and positivity, the heart rhythmic pattern is harmonic. This harmonic pattern is in perfect harmony with nature that matches the wavelengths of colours and gentle music and ensures a healthy body. We can detect a lie by measuring a person's heartbeat instead of brain signals.

Over the years, we have experimented with different psychological and physiological measures, but it was consistently heart rate variability or heart rhythms that stood out as the most dynamic and accurate reflection of the inner emotional state and stress. It becomes clear that negative emotions lead to increased disorder in the heart's rhythm and in the autonomic nervous system, thereby adversely affecting the rest of the body.

In contrast, positive emotions create increased harmony and coherence in heart rhythms and improve balance in the nervous system. Disharmony in the nervous system leads to inefficiency and increased stress on the heart and other organs while harmonious rhythms are more efficient and less stressful to the body's systems.

So, unlike the popular belief, besides pumping blood the heart also has an intelligence of its own.

According to neuro - cardiologists, 60 to 65% of heart cells are neuron cells instead of normal muscle cells. Neurons are the same cells that constitute our brain. Scientists have discovered that the heart possesses its own intrinsic nervous system.

This discovery has helped them conduct experiments that have proved the heart works similar to the brain; it can independently sense and process information.

The heart neurons can have short term and long term memory

and there is a constant exchange of information that takes place between the brain and the heart. The heart also has its own independent hormone gland that secretes several hormones and neurotransmitters that profoundly affect the body functions.

So, a human being can truly feel and think with his heart. But what has been found interesting is that in some ways the heart is even superior to the brain.

Contrary to the obvious conclusion that the human heart is bound by the signals from the brain, the fact is quite the opposite. It is, in fact, the human brain which acts in accordance to the signals released by the heart.

So if your heart feels disturbed, the effect is reflected in your brain activities in the form of stress. This information tells us that the brain is secondary to the heart.

In ancient Egypt, during the process of mummification, people used to leave the heart in the body for use in the next birth and discard the brain as a vestigial organ. This was because they believed that the heart is directly connected with the fourth and fifth sheaths called the Vigyanamaya Kosh or the Wisdom Sheath and the Anandamayi Koshor the Blissful Sheath respectively.

This was because while the Brain depends upon the inputs provided by the Indriyans, the feelings and memories generated by the heart are a result of its direct interaction with nature's consciousness.

If some other human being is in misery, the heart may feel his pain and direct the brain to help that person. This way the heart is directly getting influenced by the universal consciousness that is all around it.

The heart is the centre of Unity Consciousness and the brain is the centre of Duality Consciousness. The heart is receptive of all of nature's vibrations around a person and acts as a memory store for relationships that a person cultivates in his lifetime.

Through the hidden power of the heart, we can achieve

universal understanding; therefore, living in a world filled with peace and love is possible.

I realised my ignorance in not considering the heart in my pursuit of God. That was the mistake I was doing all along till now.

I was trying to find God through the brain realizing little that the brain itself is duality. To truly find God, I will have to find him through the heart. The heart is the gateway to the divine.

When a person values someone else more than himself, love happens. It is a feeling where that person unknowingly dissolves his own ego for the other person. On doing that, he overcomes all the restrictions imposed by h is brain over his Consciousness and outgrows beyond his physical self.

A mere presence of a loving person can comfort the one being loved in times of difficulty. That is the way love has been prophesied in all the religions as the most powerful emotion of the universe.

When a person dies, all emotions connected with that person like hate, jealousy, greed etc also vanish. All emotions except one; Love. Love is a truly multi - dimensional emotion. It starts even before a person is born and remains even after the death of that person. Even God connects with his devotees with this one emotion alone.

As Marich was lifting Rohan and Vani by their necks, I felt a synchronisation taking place in the vibrations produced by the hearts of these two lovers. Their heartbeats compounded to produce a resonance that grew stronger with each passing moment.

'I do not fear you,' Vani said, looking into the eyes of Marich.' You killed Naina but you are still scared of her reflections in me.'

'Neither do I fear you,' Rohan said.' What good is all the power and wealth if you could not make even a single person fall in love with you?'

Even while hanging in mid - air, Rohan extended and held

Vani's hand.

Marich grumbled in angst at their comments and threw both of them on the ground. Vani started bleeding profusely from her forehead.

As Marich stepped forward towards Vani, Rohan leapt and lied on top of Vani to cover her underneath himself.

Marich in his effort to lift Rohan from top of Vani, dug his nails and took out a piece of flesh from Rohan's shoulder. Rohan hugged Vani tightly into his chest.

Marich picked up the iron Trishul and charged to pierce it through the hearts of the embracing lovers in one blow but instantly, as if cast into a statue, Marich remained fixed in that state. He neither moved forward nor flinched an eyelid. He just stood there.

The battle that Marich was fighting outside had initiated a more significant inner battle inside him. It was the inner battle between his heart and mind.

CHAPTER 29

EGO

To the bewilderment of Takshak, a half - conscious carcass of Shiv was lifted hundreds of feet into the air by a jet of water, then his body was brought down and Shiv perfectly stood on the pillar of water in front of Takshak.

'I see that you have got help,' takshak said.' You can control the sea.'

'What you cannot see is that it is not my desire to control that is helping me.' Shiv opened his eyes while saying this. 'It is my willingness to surrender to the lap of nature that empowers me.'

Sarvan had taken Jal - Samadhi. He was neither living nor dead. He had just extended his identity from his body to the entire ocean which now became his new identity.

I could feel Sarvan dancing with the waves of water. I could feel his childish friskiness on the sea surface and his spiritual calmness into the depths of the ocean. I could feel a reflection of his emotions in the froth of the waves and the nurture of his benevolence in the perseverance of oceanic life.

The limited human Consciousness of Sarvan had now formed a part of the sprawling Consciousness of the sea. Sea was the place where all his fears had ended and now, he resided in the heart of the sea.

Every droplet of the sea had come alive from the memory of Sarvan's Consciousness preserved in the molecular structure of oceanic water. It was an irony that the person who once wanted to end his life would one day end up making his life unending.

Sarvan had sacrificed himself to the lap of nature in favour of the greater good, and in the process, nature had accepted the honest Soul as a part of itself. He was free. He was blissful. He was Immortal.

Takshak took out a shankh(conch) from under his golden belt and blew it. A loud deafening sound reverberated through the sky.

The crusading army of serpentine men stopped at their places on listening to the sound and turned back. The vimana's dominating the skies turned to gather at the fight scene of Takshak and Shiv.

'If you have the support of nature,' takshak said 'I have an entire army who has been hungry for this day.'

With a motion of Shiv's hand, two streams of seawater condensed into pointed icicles and shot towards Takshak.

Takshak dodged the ice bullets with his sword.

The vimana's turned towards Shiv and rained an array of a deadly stream of energy. Streams of water erupted around Shiv to engulf the fire of those deadly rays.

The battle grew intense with thousands of serpentine men returning to the beach in support of their king and hundreds on vimanas covering the sky around Shiv, raining havoc with their rays.

A dome of seawater engulfed Shiv from all around and Shiv further reinforced it with his own energy field.

The dome then erupted like a volcano, releasing thousands of icicle bullets in all directions causing some damage to the vimanas and some casualties among the serpentine men.

Then Shiv motioned the giant wall of water to fall towards the seashore.

When the wave subsided it had engulfed the complete shore drowning thousands of serpentine men.

Takshak threw his sword and took out a giant golden bow. He whispered some mantra to the bow and an arrow appeared. He mounted the arrow on the bow and shot into the sea.

A series of whirlpools appeared at the point of impact in the sea and travelled into all directions swirling the seawater in the process and forcing the sea to retreat from the shore.

Takshak shot another arrow that emitted an enormous flame of fire that burned a hole through the sea and evaporated zillions of gallons of water into the air.

Some serpentine men reappeared from beneath the sea and took out their bow and arrows to attack the ocean on the direction of their king.

'The ocean won't help you this time son of Devas,' takshak shouted.' Look at my huge army; we will rule even if we have to burn down this entire ocean.'

Shiv lifted up his hands towards the sky and communicated with me.' Do you remember that last story that Rohan's mother had told me about Lord Krishna?' Shiv asked.

'Yes, I do,' I said.

'I have understood its meaning,' Shiv said to me.

'What meaning?' I asked.

Shiv did not answer back to me. He lowered his hands and a giant wave appeared. Shiv rode the top of that wave and travelled till Takshak.

'That is one thing you have not understood even after thousands of years of struggle,' Shiv said to Takshak. 'It doesn't matter if have an infinite army on your side or unfathomable weapons in your armoury because KRISHNA IS ON MY SIDE,' Shiv said with a smile.

I could sense a change happening inside Shiv's head and this time,I knew what was happening. Shiv had passed the final test. His Rudra Granthi had opened up.

The powerful beat created by the resonance of the joint heartbeats of Rohan and Vani had created aturm oil inside

Marich'sheart. The battle had shifted from the physical world to a metaphysical dimension inside Marich and I could witness it all.

The strong impulse of love released by the emotions of Rohan and Vani had triggered a series of impulses from Marich's heart to his brain. But Marich's brain was already under the captivity of another formidable opponent - Ego.

The realisation of a Soul, that it is a physical human form defined by flesh and bone is the primary form of ego; hence, ego is a basic ingredient in the process of creation of human life. It makes a Soul aware of its body.

Ego is important, for without ego, a human being will realize himself just as a cluster of energies and civilisation as we know it would never exist. Ego gives a person an identity and with an identity come desires. These human desires then lead to the development of civilisations and social norms. The world we see around us is a by - product of human aspirations and desires that led them to dream, innovate, and discover incredible things that the world is full of.

Within a limit, egois an amazingly positive virtue. But when ego surpasses its limit, it becomes toxic.

When a man identifies with himself, he also develops a tendency to possess for himself. If there is me, then there must be something that belongs to me and so, he begins possessing by saying statements like my land, my house, my dog, my family, my money, my country, etc. But the problem with possession is that someone will always have something more than you and the one who will have maximum will always live with the fear of losing.

This further gives rise to jealousy.

It happens when a human being identifies with his limited form and competes with the limited form of other human beings to possess temporary and unessential things which are in limited supply in nature.

Jealousy is an unhealthy competition because it can only

happen for grossly unessential things which further misguide the human aim in life and divert them towards suffering. For possession of essential things which are in unlimited supply in nature, there is never a jealous factor between human beings.

So, to prove their superiority humans compete with each other by comparing their possessions. The one having more possessions will win; whatever that means. But how can we compare the possessions when nature is full of diversity and uniqueness? After all, nature follows the Law of Originality. Who can be called superior amongst three men each having a cow, a horse, and a dog respectively?

Since it was difficult to compare the enormous variety of possessions and find out who is the winner of this crap collection, humans devised an innovative way to quantify all the diversity and uniqueness of nature with a single term called money and under a single system called economy.

Economy is a system under which if a group of people decide that a horse costs more money than,say, a cow, then the rest entire mankind possessing a horse is considered to possess more compared to the rest of the mankind possessing a cow.

So, if say 1 kilogram wheat is cheaper than say 1 kilogram wood, then the person having wood is considered more blessed than the person having wheat. It doesn't matter if wheat is the basic requirement to fulfil hunger.

This is so because the economy has been born out of a human desire for competition with other humans. It is a contest which could as well be called 'possessor of maximum rarest material will be considered winner contest'.

So, if in nature, say gold is rarer than iron, then the possessor of more gold is the winner and will be considered to have a bigger ego than the possessor of iron. The utility of the possession does not matter; only the rarity matters. Needless to say that items essential for life like air, water etc have no value as they are too abundant to be possessed.

It's a competition between egos in which a person gets to be defined only by his possessions. He believes that the only aim of his life is to collect more possessions and gradually, his possessions become his identity.

Humans believe that they can gain immortality by collecting these possessions. So, if a person with the name 'Ghosh' will collect these possessions, he can gain immortality as even after his death, the name Ghosh will continue to prevail.

Human beings can go to any extent for the remembrance of their names after their death. Every single crime committed and all the bloodshed in numerous wars was done by greedy people solely to gain these possessions so that they could be remembered by their possessions long after their death.

This human desperation for Immortality and the innovative technique, could have been considered as agenius human invention but humans failed on two accounts. Either they failed to understand the purpose of human life or they failed to understand that the alive part of them was already Immortal.

Marich was also engulfed by a similar desire to give a name to his ego. He was either fighting to immortalize someone's name or wanted his name to stay after his death.

For human beings,ego might just be a feeling, but for me, it was a real red monster that remains in constant turmoil with me to gain control of the human brain. Ego gets fuelled by anger as I had experienced in my first human body of Raghu. In fact, ego can fill a person with so much anger and hatred that it can even cut me off completely from the human brain.

Marich's ego had filled him with so much anger, hatred, and desperation that it had blocked his Consciousness out of his brain. Marich had no connection with human feelings as without their Consciousness, no human being can connect with human feelings or get the correct guidance between right and wrong.

His brain was covered under the reddish layer that took a devilish shape as soon as Consciousness tried to connect to him. I could not have a chance against this strong ego of Marich by myself, but this time, I had help; it was Marich's heart.

'Whenever human beings meet other human beings, there is an interaction which takes place between their Consciousness' which remains unknown to them.

It is the result of this interaction due to which they may like or dislike each other. Even prior to their verbal interaction, their hearts can assess if they can synchronize their rhythm or not.

The impulse of Rohan and Vani's heartbeat was shaking the neurons of Marich's heart, which in turn was releasing numerous instructions for Marich's brain that weakened his ego.

And I was there in the metaphysical dimension standing in front of Marich's ego.

'You have to allow him to be human again,' I told Marich's ego, which had taken the form of a red beast now.

'I am what makes him human,' Marich's ego told me. 'It's you who confuses humans by polluting their minds with glimpses of dimensions beyond their reach.'

'The essence of human life is to explore the miracles of human Consciousness. It is only by way of a limited form that they can understand the limitless. Only a drop in the ocean can marvel at the size of the sprawling ocean; the ocean can never understand its own self.

Can human beings ever get mesmerised by the magnificence of the intricate and precise working of organs that form their own body? I really doubt if they can, because no one can get enthralled by himself. Not even God.

That is why creation is important. That is why diversity is created by nature. So that everything in nature can get enthralled by everything else around it.

So that they can wonder over the magic that lays all around them, and finally, after they have cuddled and enjoyed and admired all the beauty and care that nature has to offer, they can return to their original infinite form.

That is why everything in nature has been intermingled together with a web of Consciousness, so that they can feel each other and reverberate in the melody created by the resonance of their vibrations,' I said.

'But why did God create humans at all if they have to have a temporary existence?' Ego asked.

'Because of the law of duality; without creation, there cannot be a creator. Without something temporary in comparison, there cannot be a concept of permanent. If everything was infinite, then there will not be anyone to call it infinite; for infinite to exist, there has to be something finite in comparison.

Even for God to exist there has to be a human who can worship God, understand his grandeur, and christen the status of God to him. Without creation, if everything is God, then there will be no God,' I said.

'Then why do you worry if I give humans an identity and a hope of Immortality?' Ego said.

'Because the illusion you create diverts them from the path of happiness and contentment and leads them to nothing other than suffering and misery. You createan insatiable greed in humans that brings destruction upon mankind and nature,' I said.

'You have your existence and I have mine,' Ego said to me,' you do your thing and I will do mine.'

'This time you have taken your thing too far,' I said.' Here our paths cross.'

'You can't stop me now, can you?' Ego said, seemingly smiling at me.

'He can't but we can.' We both turned to the direction of the sound to find another bluish - white gaseous figure in the realm. I recognised it at once. She was Naina's Consciousness.

The Consciousness of two people in love synchronizes to similar wavelength that allows them to perceive the world with a similar viewpoint.

Naina's Consciousness mixed with mine to create a blazing union of duality into unity. The simmering mixture of my blue with her white, once again released a pattern of glow in which it was impossible for Ego to exist.

Marich's ego repulsed and tightened its grip over his brain.

As Rohan hugged Vani more intimately, Marich's heart intensified its tussle against his brain by releasing signals of compassion.

'You know you cannot finish me,' Ego cried.' Once a person has developed an inflated ego, then whatever you may do, it will surface again because it becomes the nature of that person. I have ruled over Marich for years and influenced every decision that he has taken.

Your control over Marich's heart will help you only for some time. When Rohan and Vani will separate, this spell you are casting over Marich will break and I will be back,' EGO said.

Vani took the lead in replying this time. 'You know, we do not intend to finish you; we just intend to control you. Once a person learns to control ego and gets guided by his Consciousness instead, he will forever aspire to be guided by his Consciousness again. Ego just survives when a person is ignorant about the presence of Consciousness. If ego is removed even for a single decision in a person's life and the person follows the path shown by his Consciousness, he will grow over this ignorance. A touch of truth is all it takes to convert a monster into a saint.'

The resonance of the combined heartbeats of Rohan and Vani were emitting strong vibrations of love that was preventing Marich from killing those two lovers. Marich's heart was sending strong messages tohis brain that was hampering the decision - making capability of his brain. The joint Consciousness of Shiv and Vani stood defiant before the subjugated Ego of Marich.

Deep inside Marich's heart lay the guilt of murdering Naina and tormenting his own child. His life was hollow despite all the possessions he had acquired. In Vani he saw Naina and in Rohan, he saw Shiv. A new reality was dawning upon him ever since he had the interaction with Takshak. A reality, that his desire to be a master of human race has only led to him being enslaved by the Nag race.

What had he done? What had he been doing throughout his life? Why couldn't he understand a simple fact that life is not about winning or losing? Life is just an experience; a chance to witness the grandeur of nature, to feel the magnificence of the divine, to discover the infinite within oneself.

The monster inside him was losing to the awakening ignited by his heart. Ego was getting diluted by his Consciousness. He had followed Aghora like a disciple throughout his life, but now, the originality of Marich was taking the lead. Without fear and without remorse, his Consciousness was rising.

Outside in the physical world, Aghora was bewildered at this hesitation on the part of Marich in piercing the Trishul through the bodies of the two embracing lovers.

'Do it!' Aghora yelled.' Finish these scumbags now.'

Marich just stood there like a statue with his arm pulling the Trishul back.

A tear rolled out of Rohan's eye onto Vani's forehead.

'We are the race of Asura's remember,' Aghora shouted.' We have to rule over these Mortal humans and defeat the Devas.'

Marich just stood there like a statue as if he had become oblivious to whatever Aghora was speaking.

'Fine. If you cannot do it, then I will do it,' Aghora said furiously.

Aghora picked up a huge rock and lifted it up over his head. He moved forward to crush Rohan and Vani under the boulder.

'I will not allow anything that can prevent the end of humanity,' Aghora yelled, as he raised the boulder in the air.

Vani held Rohan's face in her hands and kissed him.

At the pulse of the moment, Marich swung his hand holding the Trishul in a circular motion. The tip of the Trishul accelerated in the air making a clean slit across the throat of Aghora.

Aghora stumbled for a moment and fell on the ground. The boulder fell on top of Aghora's head, crushing him completely.

The Consciousness of love had won the battle against the ego of hate inside Marich's head. Marich's heart had won over his brain. I had won half the battle against evil with the power of human heart, the balance half would be fought with the pineal gland.

CHAPTER 30

GOD

'Do you remember that last story that Rohan's mother told me?' Shiv's voice drew my attention towards a greater battle that was ensuing at the other front.

'Are you talking about the story of Barbarika?' I asked.

'Barbarika was the son of Ghatothkach and the grandson of Bhima. He was the most powerful warrior in the war of Mahabharata and had three infallible arrows granted by Lord Shiva with which he could finish the war within a few minutes. But he made a promise to his mother to fight on the side of the losing team.

Lord Krishna knew the power of Barbarika and realised that as the battle will swing, Barbarika will keep switching to fight from the losing side until he destroys both sides of the armies and come out as the lone survivor of the war.

So, he asked Barbarika to sacrifice his head before the war. Barbarika agreed with the request that he should be allowed to watch the entire battle of Mahabharata.

Lord Krishna granted his wish by placing his severed head on top of a hill overlooking the battlefield and gave him the name 'Khatu Shyamji' and a blessing that he will be worshipped as the 'God of Kali - yuga'.

After the battle of Mahabharata, the Pandavas had an argument over who amongst them was most responsible for the victory.

Since Barbarika had watched the complete war, they all went to Barbarika and asked their query.

Barbarika replied that throughout the duration of the battle, he could neither see Pandavas or Kaurvas. He only saw Sudarshan Chakra (the weapon of Lord Krishna) flying everywhere and slaying the wrong doers on both sides and establishing Dharma (the rule of righteousness).

Pandavas and Kauravas were mere instruments or mediums through which Lord Krishna had created this Leela (divine play) called Mahabharata,' Shiv said.

'What does that mean?' I asked.

'Now remember that painting in which a scene of Mahabharata was depicted in which Lord Krishna the charioteer is standing in the middle of the two armies and explaining Dharma in the form of Geeta (the divine song) to Arjuna,' Shiv said.

'Yes, I clearly remember that it had Lord Hanuman also sitting on top of Arjuna's chariot.'

'Can you find a correlation between the two stories?' Shiv asked.

I pondered at the question asked by Shiv.

'If the chariot is the human body being pulled by its five senses depicted as horses and Arjuna is the Soul then Lord Krishna is the God who is directly steering the Soul to its destined path,' I said.

'Correct. So if I am Arjuna, then who are you?' Shiv asked.

I was flabbergasted for a moment; all this while, I could not see this obvious correlation.

Chit appearing to guide me as my friend was no accident. He was always there, just like Lord Hanuman sits on top of Arjuna's chariot.

That leaves Me in the role of Lord Krishna, guiding the chariot of Shiv in the direction of his destiny.

'But how can this be possible? How can I be playing the role of God? God is the knower of everything and I have been desperately seeking advice from several people including you, Shiv,' I told Shiv.

'Don't you realize it?' Shiv continued,' All along it was you who was guiding the destinies of five strangers into each other. It was you who fought Marich and Aghora through different human bodies. It was you who gained Siddhis as you gained knowledge about yourself.

I, Sarvan, or Rohan were just instruments through which you were playing, but the game was always yours.

In the twists that have taken place, you have played arole similar to the one played by Lord Krishna in the battle of Mahabharata. The only difference is that he could be seen in his physical form and you cannot be seen.

All the family members hail me for they think I have got superpowers, but in my heart, I know that it is you who is making all this possible and not me,' Shiv said.

'But there have been many instances when I have taken guidance from you, Shiv,' I said, remembering the moments when I was full of self - doubts.

'When you say "Shiv", do you mean Shiv–the body, Shiv–the brain, or Shiv–the mind?' Shiv replied.

It stunned me for a while.

Shiv was right. Who have I been talking to all this while?

All along the journey, I had been communicating with the different human bodies that I resided in and I interacted with them without realising that it is only Me what is alive inside human bodies. If I am the one seeking advice, then who was the one replying back?

AND THEN THERE WAS' LIGHT'.

As if thousands of suns had suddenly illuminated the darkness inside Shiva's head, the dark confines in which I was used to limiting my existence dissolved into infinity extending till as far as I could see.

A sound of 'Om' started reverberating from nowhere to everywhere.

Inside Shiv's body, the Kundalini had completed its ascent till

Ajna Chakra. The Kundalini had risen through the five lower chakras depicting elements of Earth, water, fire, air, and ether and entered into the realm of light.

The Ajna Chakra is symbolized by a violet lotus with two petals. It is located directly behind the forehead. It is the seat of Consciousness as well as our sixth sense, often referred to as the Psychic Chakra. The deity associated with this region is Ardha - Narishvara, an androgynous form of Shiva - Shakti, symbolizing the duality of male and female energies. The two petals represent the primordial duality of subject and object, otherwise known as the psychic channels, Ida and Pingala. These two channels merge with the central channel, Sushumna, signifying the end of duality.

With the Kundalini entering the Ajna Chakra, one learns how to see beyond the five body senses by trumping the ego with the cosmic mind. The individual ego gets merged with the cosmicego and the egocentric self becomes the cosmic infinite self. This is where awareness expands to the realization that nothing is separate, that we are truly all one.

Ajna means to command. Through the sixth chakra and the pineal gland, we can master our minds. The third eye allows us to have a clear perception of our reality. It coordinates the activity of the pineal gland and of the cerebellum.

The opening of Shiv's Ajna Chakra was a surreal experience and difficult to describe.

The illumination caused by the white light enabled me to see the reality beyond reality. Even with closed eyes, I could see the complete scene as it was playing outside.

I saw Takshak and thousands of serpentine men standing with all the natural features around them.

And I saw more than that. I could see through beyond their physical bodies.

Slowly, their physical bodies got dissolved into just the five primary elements that comprised them.

I could see the predominance of water (liquid) element in

every living thing and the predominance of Earth (solid) in every non - living entity. I saw the air element filling up the cavities to regulate the flow of Prana in every living entity. I saw the fire (energy) element energising life into every single thing around. And then there was space (element). It was just a void filled with nothingness.

I saw the five sheaths of a human body clearly discernible from one other. I had always wondered what would lie underneath the Anandamaya Kosh or the bliss sheath. I got the answer today. There was nothing. It was purely empty from inside. There was no Soul or God or anything else residing within it. I understood the wisdom of the talk that my guru, Rohan's mother, had imparted me with.

99% of space inside an atom is nothing. 99% of the Universe that we live in comprises of nothing; some scientists also call it dark energy.

If mathematics is the language in which God has written the universe, then Shunya (Zero) is the number by which nothing has been described.

When God creates a ray of light, then he creates that ray of light in an infinite nothingness. Every creation is born out of nothing and gets dissolved back into nothing.

God is this nothing which is everything. What has been created is always finite, but what has not been created is infinite. Nothingness is the infinite form of God.

Gradually, even the five elements that I was seeing disappeared and what finally remained was just a cluster of energies interwoven with each other to give shape to the five elements.

Then slowly, even the bundle of energies subsided and manifested into sound. Everything that I saw around me a while back gradually disappeared into just a sound wave similar to the sound of Damru (pellet drum). The Damru held by Lord Shiva is not just a musical instrument. It is a symbol of creation in the hands of the God of destruction.

The picture of Natraj flashed in my mind. It is a depiction of

Tandav; the dance of destruction by Lord Shiva.

In the picture, Lord Shiva is surrounded by a circle of fire depicting destruction all around him. There is a child under his feet symbolizing creation that is getting destroyed. The palm of his left hand is facing in front as if blessing the person watching the picture and with his right hand, he is motioning downwards towards his feet, under which the child is getting crushed. It seems as if Lord Shiva were saying that I am blessing the child of ignorance by destroying his limited creation and remerging him with the infinite.

Then there are two more hands that are depicted.

With another right hand, he is holding a Trishul symbolising destruction; and with another left hand, he is holding a Damru symbolising creation. Both these hands are kept perfectly at the same level to convey that creation and destruction are taking place together.

Then I noticed the presence of a bluish glow in all the living things around me. Whether it be trees or humans or the army of Asuras or the ocean, there was a mild bluish glow similar to me.

As all the living and non - living entities around me disappeared, only this mild bluish glow remained. Rest everything got dissolved into the white light and finally into the sound of Damru.

And then I noticed something outlandish.

I noticed a thin bluish line that was emanating from within me and extending outwards. On closer scrutiny, I realised that there is a blueish thread that was coming out of every single piece of creation whether living or non - living. What was more was that these bluish threads were all converging into each other as they extended outwards.

I tried to reach out to the end of these threads only to find it to be unending and infinite.

And then, finally, the spectacular scene unfolded before my eyes.

The white sheet of light merged into a huge bluish figure. All the bluish threads merged into that bluish figure. The bluish figure was infinite and towered in front of me like a sky with no end.

Billions and billions of blueish threads were all emanating from him and dissolving back into him.

Slowly, the infinite and shapeless blue began taking a form.

I recognised the enormous form of Lord Vishnu in an instant. I noticed millions of galaxies all dissolving into his form and million others taking birth.

The soundof Shiva's Damru was giving shape to billions of creations in the light of Vishnu's body. The light that illuminated this creation was nothing but his body.

'The seeker shall find.' I remembered these words of Chit and was overwhelmed by the thought of my quest for God finally reaching its conclusion.

I realised the truth. I realised who I was. I was nothing but a tiny particle that comprised the body of Lord Vishnu. And like me, there were billions of particles with every single particle having an independent body either living or non - living.

Every single particle was the source of life in the body that it was supporting. Lord Vishnu was present in everything in nature in equal measure. And everything in nature totalled upto the body of Lord Vishnu.

And it was the body of Lord Vishnu itself which was termed' Universal Consciousness'.

The individual Consciousness present in every human being was not only a tiny fragment of the enormous Universal Consciousness but they were all connected with each other. In fact, they just appeared like cells of the same body.

'As outside so inside.' I realised the mystery of these words. Everything that a human being sees outside was nothing but the body of Lord Vishnu and everything that resides inside him is Me; the same body of Lord Vishnu.

If I know everything that happens in the body that I reside in, then Lord Vishnu also knows everything that happens in billions of living entities. That is why he is said to have billions of eyes through which he sees and billions of hands through which he works. He was the doer and also what has been done.

I realised that whichever path of destiny I took, it wouldn't matter. The path a human being follows is pre - decided. Because whatever thoughts and experiences I was having were being fed to me by Lord Vishnu himself.

Sometimes he guided me as Chit and sometimes he helped me out as Naina and sometimes confronted me as Marich, but overall, it was just a divine play or Leela taking place.

I bowed down to the colossal and divine form of Lord Vishnu and realised the truth. It was the same truth that Arjuna must have realised after seeing the divine form of Lord Krishna.

The Truth was that this world is a divine play synchronised to a divine tune, and all we can do is just play our parts; cause if we don't, then also we will play our parts.

The light slowly disappeared and I soon returned to my limited human Consciousness form.

Marich was lying pale in a semi - conscious state on the floor. He had shrunken in size and looked old and frail. The death of Aghora had broken the spell that kept Marich youthful and strong.

'What I have brought upon Earth cannot be undone!' Marich spoke in a feeble voice. Rohan and Vani came close to Marich.

'I would choose to reframe your sentence,' Vani said,' what you have brought on Earth cannot be undone, without the will of God.'

'Many men have lived their lives thinking they were invincible. They lived with a dream of world domination and some even convinced the rest of the world about their capabilities. But finally, it is the will of God that prevails,' Vani said.

Rohan walked to the Shiva idol at the centre of the temple. The iPad with the control of all the frequencies that were being released to control the population was kept there. Rohan turned the knobs to switch off all the frequencies.

As the frequencies stopped, millions of people sitting around water and chanting the mantra's instantly grew quiet as if woken up from a dream.

The great Yagna had ended.

With the end of the great Yagna, the power from the sound of chants ceased and the immense strength of Asura's dried up because the source chants ceased of their strength wasthe sound created by the chants.

'Barbarika was right,' I said. 'It was Lord Krishna on both sides. It is just the way of establishing Dharma back in the world by slaying the ignorant and their ignorance with the Sudarshan Chakra.'

Through Shiv's eyes, I saw Takshak shooting his next arrow upwards into the air. Along with him, hundreds of serpentine men also fired their arrows towards Shiv.

The hail of arrows covered the entire sky like a cloud and descended upon Shiv.

Shiv closed his eyes and looked up towards the sky. But this time even with closed eyes, his sight was not lost.

This time instead of Me looking through Shiv's eyes, Shiv was looking through my eyes. The duality of sight had ended.

Even with closed eyes, I could see everything exactly as it was happening outside.

Shiv felt a pain in his head. The Shree - Yantra embedded with Neelum appeared to me as an infinite pyramidal paradox that was channelizing energy from the universe into the blue sapphire stone rooted exactly at the stem centre of the Shree - Yantra.

The blue sapphire crystal was, in turn, focusing the entire energy in the form of a beam of blue light and projecting it through the middle of the two lobes of the brain directly onto the pineal gland.

The realization of my infinite form and the sensation of nearness to Krishna had removed all traces of worry from me. I felt fearless and invincible.

The ray of blue light that was focussed on the pineal gland in Shiv's brain was igniting the power produced by Kundalini that was now residing in Shiv's Ajna Chakra.

The pain inside Shiv's head intensified as the rain of arrows accelerated downwards to pierce through his body.

I saw the layer of ego on Shiv's brain completely disappear for a moment. I felt as if his brain had turned into an active volcano about to erupt into a shower of molten lava.

I was right. Shiv's brain exploded.

The normally upward - looking third eye called the pineal gland moved till it focussed in front of the forehead in the direction of the blue ray of light.

The next instant, just before the arrows were about to touch his body,a blinding light appeared out of Shiv's pineal gland.

The ray of light was so intense and so horrifying that it was nothing like what I had seen till now. It evaporated the rain of arrows in an instant and pierced a hole in the sky.

Shiv's Third Eye had opened.

Shiv turned his head around towards the sprawling army of Asuras. Where ever he looked, he burned everything he laid his eyes upon. In an instant, the mighty race of Nag Asuras was reduced to ashes. Within minutes the battlefield transformed. The magnificent vimanas erupted like balls of fire and the giant serpents scattered into bits and pieces.

Nothing could escape from the destruction he brought. Every tactic of the enemy failed. Every move by the Asuras backfired. Shiv had turned into death itself. Shiv had turned into a human manifestation of the' God of Destruction'.

The slaughter continued till Takshak was the only one standing. He was standing in stunned silence at the sudden turn of events.

The ray disappeared from Shiv's forehead.

'Who are you? How do you have the powers of Mahadev Lord Shiva?'takshak asked.

'I am Shiv,son of Naina and Marich. That's all I know,' Shiv said, after humbling down.

'But it is impossible for a human to have these powersunless… 'takshak paused for a while and got lost in deep contemplation.

'I bow down to you,' takshak said after recovering.

'What is that you know about me King Takshak?' Shiv asked.

'I think I will leave that mystery for you to unravel by yourself,' takshak said. 'I now understand the grand plan of God. It was beyond my wildest imagination but I am now in awe of it. If you have come this far, God will guide you further in the path of self - discovery.'

'What kind of self - discovery?' Shiv asked.

'There are secrets far beyond what you have discovered so far, Shiv,' takshak said.' secrets that lay beyond the confines of this world or universe. Secrets that have the potential to change the course of mankind. Secrets that were known to mankind once but were forgotten when this age of ignorance and deception set in.

Your Kundalini Shakti has reached the sixth chakra but you know what,the Sushumna Nadi ends at the sixth chakra. There is no pathway available for your Kundalini Shakti to further ascent till Sahasrara Chakra.

I had recognised you the first instant I saw you. But you are yet to discover yourself fully. I believe that it is your destiny to find your purpose and in the process, change the future of mankind.

There is still a final chapter that you will have to unravel in this path.

If you think I was bad, then you will have to wait till you see the real demon. All I can say is that I have understood what my role was in this divine play. My role is complete. All you have to do is complete your role.

It is my time to go,' takshak said and turned back to the sea.

'But I have just killed your complete army,' Shiv intertwined.

'Death is a human concept created due to the illusion of time,' takshak said, as he picked up his sword and kept it back in its sheath.

'Think. What if there was no concept of Time?

No age limit. Nothing would ever take birth. Nothing would ever die. Without time,there cannot be speed; so all kinds of motion would stop. Without time,there cannot be a concept of space; so nothing would appear near or far.

Would possessions have any worth if you are destined to live forever? No rules can be made for an Immortal society. There would be no need for God to protect you from hell. All the religions would vanish from the face of Earth. You humans would end your greed for possession. You would stop worshipping God. When you live a life without the concept of time, reality becomes clearer.

We are Immortals. You have killed nothing. Nothing ever dies. You have just sent my army back to the place it came from,and it is my time to join them.'

With this Takshak slithered into the sea and disappeared in an instant.

The next instant, I felt a force pulling me out of Shiv's mind. I felt as if the entire cosmos around me was collapsing. Everything around started to revolve in a spiral motion around me as if trying to enter me.

Then suddenly, everything went dark and there was a momentary calm as if time had come to a standstill. It was the calm after the storm. The vengeance unleashed by the destructive forces of nature by razing the unnatural manmade structure to ground is an act of restoration of the natural order. The disappearance of the Asuras left behind a wake of genocide and destruction, but before I could assimilate my loss or appreciate my victory, I was forced into another awakening. The one I had forgotten so far.

CHAPTER 31

THE AWAKENING

I opened my eyes to find myself in a hospital with a queue of patients standing in front of me.

'Maybe Shiv fainted and someone got him to a hospital,' I thought.

The scene of mass murder by the army of Asuras was still livid in my mind. I needed to know what happened to Rohan, Vani, and Santy. So, I jumped the queue and went straight to the reception counter.

'Excuse me, can you tell me where are they treating the survivors of the holocaust caused by Asuras on the beach of Goa?' I asked the receptionist.

The receptionist looked at me from top to down as if inspecting my attire and replied, 'You might be referring to the casualty in ward number 4; go straight down the corridor and take the first left, you will find him.'

There was a survivor.

I ran down to ward number 4 and opened the door. A group of people were sitting around a middle - aged man with a plastered leg. This was not what I was hoping to find. Nevertheless, I went to him to strike a conversation.

'Hey, can you describe happened after the massacre at Goa beach? I am searching for my friends,' I said.

All the members of the group looked at me exactly in the same manner asthe receptionist. The patient finally spoke.'

What massacre? I broke my leg as the cord broke while I was paragliding in Goa. But that was two days back, now they have got me admitted in this hospital in Mumbai.'

I was stunned. It seemed as if no one knew about what happened only a few moments back. What could be the problem? Did the influence of the yagna made their memories weak or was it the calcination of their pineal glands?

I ran out of the hospital. I needed to understand what had gone wrong with mankind.

Mumbai seemed to be running on its usual leisurely pace. Not one person had a clue of what I was talking about.

While I was madly confused by the obliviousness of these people, a slight vibration in my pocket distracted my attention. It was a mobile phone.

'Where are you, Shiv? I and Vani have been waiting in your office for over an hour now, she says it is important that you see it now.' I was jubilant at recognising the familiar voice of Rohan.

'My office! Where is my office?' I asked, wondering when did Shiv acquire an office.

'Oh God, I guess you are lost again. Wait and stay put at the place you are at presently. Just send me your location on WhatsApp and I will send a car to pick you up,' Rohan said.

Shiv opened his mobile and his muscle memory knew how to send his location on WhatsApp. In about an hour, Shiv was entering the building of Tripura Pharmaceutical's Ltd. As he entered, I noticed the giant portrait of Marich hanging from the ceiling.

Shiv went straight to the reception.

'Excuse me! Can you please tell me where ismy office located?' Shiv asked.

The pretty receptionist stood up with an expression of disbelief on her face.

'Sir, you really must be joking. I will take you there myself if you have any problem,' she said.

The receptionist held Shiv's hand and took her to the top floor of the building into a huge room with glass windows. Shiv recognised the place at once. It was the same office where Marich had murdered him.

Everything was the same except, that now, the office had Shiv's portrait hanging on a wall. Rohan and Vani were sitting on a luxurious white sofa in a corner.

The reality began to dawn upon me.

Sarvan took that one life - changing decision which was to make Shiv read the Golaka Chart that the hermit had given him. That one small decision had changed the course of the timeline in the present universe and sent me into a parallel universe where I had won the battle against evil.

But the bodies I commanded were left behind in the present universe. I had fought the complete battle through the replicas of these human bodies in the other parallel Universe.

So, while my actions changed the course in the parallel universe, the effect of my Karmas also implied upon the lives of these human bodies in this universe in the form of luck or destiny.

When Marich won his internal war between Consciousness and Ego in the parallel universe, his Consciousness was able to transcend this effect across other parallel universes as well.

Hence, in the present universe, Marich handed over all his business to Shiv and moved away to repent for his evil actions and the troubles he caused to Naina.

Rohan and Vani had become close aides of Shiv in running the medicine business alongside Shiv and were extremely loyal to him. Obviously, this trust was a result of a deeper interplay between the Consciousnesses of these three individuals.

Santy had his car designing start - up funded by Shiv's business empire.

Sarvan drowned in the ocean and after being widowed, Vani had found comfort with Rohan. Humans can neither understand nor explain why they suddenly start to like someone. This time I did not feel the need to enlighten them.

The event of Asuras emerging from the underworld never happened in the present universe.

Vani came close to Shiv and kept her hand on his cheek,' You know your autism is not fully cured. You are imagining strange things. It is not good for you to venture out alone like this.' With that, she planted a gentle kiss on Shiv's forehead.

Shiv WAS AUTISTIC. He had a gift of hyperactive imagination.

This time I did not feel the need to explain to these ignorant humans that this autistic superhero had won a war against evil and changed the course of their destinies. His power was that he could understand and connect with me better than any other so - called normal person.

What they call imaginations are not just arbitrary products of the human brain. They are visualisations that their higher self has with a higher Consciousness in a higher dimension.

Imagination is the most important ability of the human mind which unfortunately has been reduced to be called a disease in the human world. Everything is imagination. Success is imagination. Sex is imagination. God is imagination.

Imagination is a reality in which a person lives. The best products of this human world are a result of the belief of a stubborn human upon his imagination. Science is imagination.

Maybe that's why it is said that the entire creation is just a dream of Vishnu. When you believe in your dream, it becomes real.

The moment was disturbed by the opening of the office door as Rohan's mother walked inside holding the Shree - Yantra in her hand.

'Shiv! Look what I have got for you,' Rohan's mother said and handed over the Shree - Yantra to Shiv.

She had fixed a Neelum at the centre of the Shree - Yantra

exactly the way she had done in the parallel universe.

Tears rolled down Shiv's eyes as he saw his guru and mother standing in front of him again. He tightly embraced her and started sobbing.

'What happened to him?' Rohan's mother inquired.' Has he been imagining weird things again? Don't worry, this Neelum will multiply the strength of this Shree - Yantra and heal his autism in no time.'

Deep inside, I understood the sarcasm. I could feel Chit smiling as he played with the words spoken through the mouth of Rohan's mother.

'We will deal with everything later,' Shiv said.' Right now I just need to spend some family time.'

CHAPTER 32

AFTERWARDS

Later that day, Shiv, Vani, and Rohan were sitting on a rock near the beach watching the sunset.

'How much do we know about ourselves?' Vani said.' We try to define the present world only on the basis of the inaccurate preliminary education imparted to us in schools and colleges.

Ironically, today's hi - tech human civilisation is based on the energy extracted out of the juices of the buried and decayed dead bodies of ancient animals that were extinct thousands of years ago.

While the ancient methods cradled civilisations for thousands of years, our modern industrial revolution has brought the world close to extinction within a hundred years.

The knowledge that modern science boasts about, is an understanding of just machines and dead objects. They are still clueless about the real laws governing nature.'

'We need to re - connect with the Mother Nature,' Rohan said, 'the society needs to be told about the truth before they enslave themselves by ignorance and deception.'

Shiv was lost in himself with his eyes closed and could clearly hear the conversation between the random thoughts in his mind.

I was still contemplating the events as it had become difficult for even me to understand if I was living reality earlier or now. The difference between real and virtual had become blurred. Maybe sometimes I should do it the way humans do it. Maybe

I should continue living in the present without trying to understand the bigger picture.

In my pursuit to find God, I had understood one simple fact. That God is not some complicated mathematical equation to be solved. It is just a devotion to be felt. The only thing that needs to be done is to feel the world from your heart rather than the mind;to look inwards rather than outside; enjoy the design of nature rather than trying to control or amend it. Leave oneself completely in the hands of God, with faith that he will take you where you are meant to go,and then enjoy the ride as he carries you.

Shiv gently opened his eyes to see Rohan and Vani in conversation with each other.' Why are you guys wasting time talking to each other when the sea is inviting you inside with open arms ready to shower its love on you,' Shiv said with a smile.

Then without another word, Shiv jumped down the rock. He moved towards Vani and removed her slippers. Then he looked up towards her

'I will be on guard, my Goddess. I will see to it that no one disturbs your privacy.'

As if understanding the secret language, Vani pushed Rohan first and then jumped down the rock. Then with a smile on her face, she came close to Shiv and handed over her bag in his hands and said,' then this time, I will ensure that I get drenched in that love.'

Vani held Rohan's hand and walked towards the sea.

As the first wave touched her feet,she could feel the warmth of Sarvan's touch. The gentle caress of waves sent electrifying sensations down her nerves. Sarvan was out there in the form of a sprawling sea playing with Vani and looking happy that his love had come to meet him.

As Vani went waist - deep into the sea, she could feel the water moistening her body with its wet kisses. For a moment, she was lost in the euphoria of the erotic sensations that the sea was enflaming inside her. The experience of true love was converging like a sexual fantasy upon her. Vani removed her clothes to feel the divine play all over her body.

A returning wave engulfed Rohan and brought her closer to Vani. Rohan emerged out of the water and held Vani in a tight embrace hugging her onto his naked torso. The sea waves submerged them till their neck creating a tingling sensation that further fuelled the fire.

As I looked through Shiv's eyes, I saw years of latent passions igniting into the three lovers, fulfilling their long - awaited desires. Sex among them looked like a cosmic union of Purush and Prakriti (Man and Nature); the synchronisation of sexual vibrations of the Mortals with the infinite; the merging of duality into unity.

BIBLIOGRAPHY

Books

Sadhguru (multiple books)

Aghora by Robert E Svoboda

Laws of the Spirit World by Khorshed Bhavnagri

Chakras by Harish Johari

I am the Mind by Deep Trivedi

Websites

www.ajitvadakayil.blogspot.in

www.hinduwebsite.com

www.yachnayoga.wordpress.com

www.worldhinduparisad.org

www.yogapedia.com

www.zenlama.com

www.bayareameditation.com

www.themagicofquantum.com

www.speakingtree.in

www.vedpuran.net

www.blog.mindvalley.com

www.en.wikipedia.org

www.skyboom1.tripod.com

www.subconsciousmethods.blogspot.com

www.binauralbeatsmeditation.com

www.powerthoughtsmeditationclub.com

www.meditativemind.org

www.world-of-lucid-dreaming.com

You Tube Channels

Swami Sarvpriyananda lectures at IIT

Hinduism lecture by Sandeep Manudhane

Cynamatics by Nigel John Stanford

Logical Hindu

Spirit Science

Magical Indian

Indian Monk

Links to addl You Tube videos

https://www.youtube.com/watch?v=O8ShNGH_RaA

https://www.youtube.com/watch?v=E-TZKiJW1UQ

https://www.youtube.com/watch?v=hy-1iY3j0M4

https://www.youtube.com/watch?v=MxvQusr9cwc

https://www.youtube.com/watch?v=ffUlDIoOynw

https://www.youtube.com/watch?v=D7eBQfM3UrA

https://www.youtube.com/watch?v=R0VPDd0JwCE

https://www.youtube.com/watch?v=QzzMktp3xR4